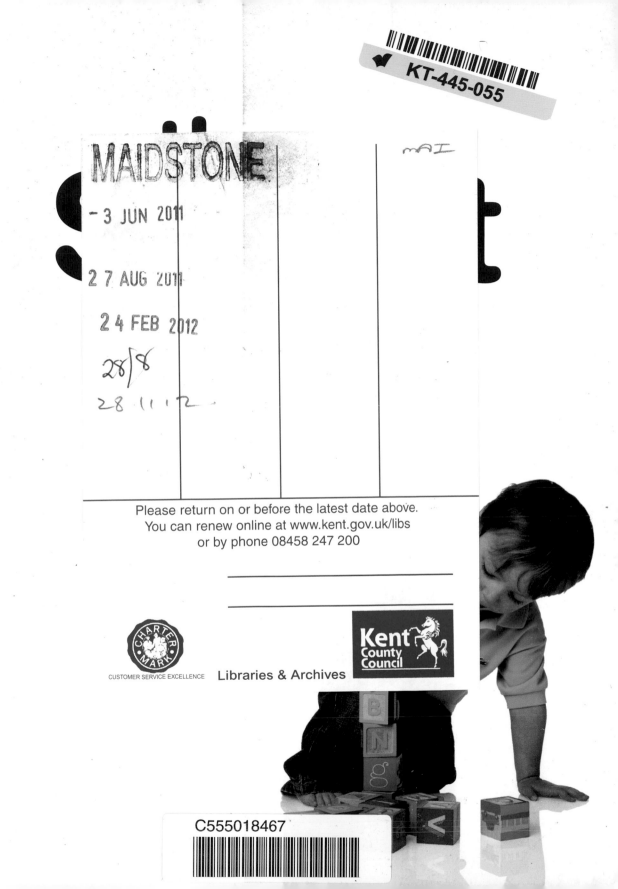

the Secret of Play

How to raise bright, healthy,
caring children from birth to age 12

Ann Pleshette Murphy

London, New York, Munich, Melbourne, Delhi

EXECUTIVE EDITOR Anja Schmidt

DESIGNER Jee Chang

ART DIRECTOR Dirk Kaufman

MANAGING ART EDITOR Michelle Baxter

DTP COORDINATOR Kathy Farias

PRODUCTION MANAGER Ivor Parker

EXECUTIVE MANAGING EDITOR Sharon Lucas

CHILD PHOTOGRAPHER Ross Whittaker

TOY PHOTOGRAPHER Ryann Cooley

ILLUSTRATOR Gabriel Pages

DOWNTOWN BOOKWORKS INC.

Produced by Downtown Bookworks Inc.

PRESIDENT Julie Merberg

SENIOR VICE PRESIDENT Pam Abrams

PRODUCTION EDITOR Sara Newberry

SPECIAL THANKS Patty Brown, Kate Gibson, Sarah Parvis

First published in Great Britain in 2008
by Dorling Kindersley Limited,
80 Strand, London WC2R 0RL

A Penguin Company

2 4 6 8 10 9 7 5 3 1

J649.5

Published in the United States by DK Publishing.

A CIP catalogue record for this book is available from the British Library.
ISBN: 978-1-4053-3789-2

Colour reproduction by Colourscan, Singapore
Printed and bound in China by Sheck Wah Tong

Discover more at
www.dk.com

Contents

Introduction

Parents know and experts agree that as our children dash and splash and squish and build and pretend their way through their early years, they're doing much more than letting off steam or burning calories. Through play children develop an understanding of who they are, make exciting discoveries about the world they live in, build their vocabularies, strengthen relationships, and experience the healing power of a shared laugh. Research tells us that play also boosts the circuits in young children's brains, impacting every aspect of their development: cognitive, emotional, physical. During their playtime, your children are forming a set of complex and flexible skills.

Unfortunately, we live in a world that too often is over-scheduled and increasingly wired, which can confound our best efforts to make unstructured play a priority. *The Secret of Play* highlights the key developmental milestones that affect the way our children play and describes the kind of play that best enhances the development of our little ones.

In every age-specific chapter, we tell you **what you'll notice** about your child's play; **why it's happening**; and, most importantly, **how to have fun with it**. You'll find research-based information on your child's learning, loving, and healthy play, plus inspiring tips from parents.

Underlying *The Secret of Play* are some important assumptions about playtime: keep it simple. Toys and games with lots of bells and whistles often deprive children of using their imaginations and engaging all their senses. Keep it safe. Children are born scientists; they need a play environment that permits plenty of adventure without constantly hearing "No!" or

"Watch out!" Follow your child's lead. As much as possible, let your child guide you during play. And when he hits a snag, encourage him to persevere. Be fully present. It's far better to commit to an uninterrupted, focused fifteen minutes of play than a half hour of distracted interaction. Get moving. Childhood obesity rates are skyrocketing. Make active, outdoor play a priority for the whole family. Make them laugh. Humour and silly games are not only essential building blocks of play; they can help you to navigate tricky terrain, like tantrums and sibling rivalry.

What you'll discover as you read this book is that play is a unique and revealing lens through which to view your child's miraculous growth – from rattle to tennis racquet, from peek-a-boo to Parcheesi. *The Secret of Play* will help you find ways to enlarge your child's world, feed his passions, boost his brain power, make him laugh, and promise him a bright, happy, sometimes silly tomorrow. Now go out and play!

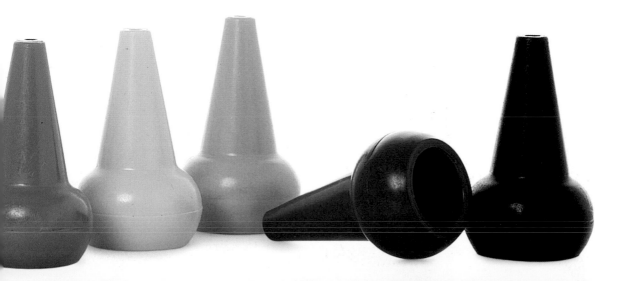

zero to twelve months
The Wonder Year

* * *

play milestones for this year

REACH for a mobile

PLAY peek-a-boo

FEEL different textures

BOND with you

KICK in a bouncy seat

FOCUS on self in a mirror

GRASP a rattle

The Wonder Year

After nine long months of waiting, your baby has arrived at last – each tiny fingernail, lock of hair, sleepy sigh, and creamy patch of skin a minor miracle. And while your long days and even longer nights after the birth will be consumed with feeding, changing, and soothing your newborn, in the blink of an eye, you will watch those tiny lips break into a smile, feel those little fingers grip onto yours, and marvel as those chubby thighs kick, crawl, stand, and, perhaps, take a few wobbly steps.

Though it will be a while before your child is hosting tea parties, rolling play dough, dressing as a superhero, scaling the monkey bars, or jumping in the mud, play is still an important part of her life. Throughout these early weeks and months the definition of play will evolve. In the first three months of life – often called the "fourth trimester" because it's a time of transition for you and your baby – play will consist simply of cuddling, talking, singing, and responding to your little one's babbles and cries. But research on infant functioning shows that between 3 and 4 months you'll see a big shift in your baby's development. She'll sleep for longer stretches at night, be able to see better and to manage stimuli – all of which means the way she plays will change, too. She will be able to focus on an object more than 20 to 30 centimetres from her face, even seeking your gaze from across the room; at 3 months, she will track an object like a stuffed animal as you move it slowly from side to side.

Soon enough, she'll show off her developing fine motor skills as she grabs, grasps, and pinches. But her hands aren't the only body parts that are getting more capable. The muscles of her tiny neck and back are developing and at about 6 to 9 months, your baby will sit up all by herself. Think you're excited? Imagine how she feels about this fresh view of her surroundings. Eager to inspect them, she'll soon be ready to go-go-go, whether that's on her bottom, knees, stomach, or tiptoes as you hold her hands.

Your baby's communication skills will also improve by leaps and bounds. Surprisingly, after mere weeks together the two of you will learn to "talk" with looks, gestures, and sounds forming the basis of your own special language. This not only bonds you deeply, but your attention to her is a source of comfort and safety, feelings that enhance all aspects of her development.

All these milestones will be met in due time, so if your baby seems slow to walk or has far fewer discernable words than her playmates next door, don't panic. Children's development is often characterized by a two-steps-forward-one-step-back progression; even siblings rarely follow the same developmental arc. (Ditto boys and girls.) What helps all babies, though, is the way their caregivers play with them. When you answer your baby's babbling, encourage her to reach for a dangling toy, read her a board book, or elicit a laugh with a well-timed raspberry to her belly, you enhance her development.

And you don't need to set aside hours of playtime to have an impact on your child's growth. Everyday routines – like bathing, feeding, and getting ready for bed – provide plenty of opportunities for play. And this everyday play will have a huge impact on your child's cognitive development and the emotional and social skills that set the groundwork for the rest of her life.

learning play

Baby talk

What you'll notice

In the beginning, newborns do what newborns do best: cry. For little ones, it's the only way they can express their needs, whether it's for food, sleep, comfort, or a desire to play. As daunting as it may be at first to distinguish a "hungry" cry from a "bored" cry, fairly soon you'll be able to decipher what she wants and how quickly you have to respond. A little whimpering in the morning may give way to contented coos once she focuses on the colourful mobile over her cot – precluding a need to rush in and pick her up.

Right from the start, you'll notice that you and your baby are learning to communicate. Several studies have shown that newborns prefer speech to other sounds – especially if Mum or Dad is doing the talking. By 5 or 6 weeks, she'll probably flash her first smile and around 3 to 6 months, get ready for your first parent-child chat as your baby babbles or coos in response to sounds or words you say. In fact, some research shows that children as young as 3 to 4 months can understand the sounds and rhythms of a conversation – staying quiet while you talk and "speaking" when you pause. Around ages 4 to 6 months, your baby may say certain sounds like "mama" or "gaga" over and over and may actually laugh if you do something she finds funny.

Towards the end of this year, you'll be amazed to see that your child understands much of what you're saying and may be able to play simple games like, "Where's your nose?" or "Find the cat in the picture". And come her first birthday, her first word – typically "Mama" or "Dada" – will undoubtedly make your day.

Why it's happening

Many linguists are convinced that the development of language is as instinctive as eating or sleeping. From birth, human babies are driven to talk. Parents of twins often discover that their babies develop a way of communicating – a kind of secret language – long before they utter their first words.

If you're the parent of a boy you may notice that he's not as garrulous as his girlfriends seem to be. Several studies have shown that girls tend to be more verbal than boys, starting to talk a month or two earlier than boys. There's even evidence that female fetuses tend to move their mouths more than males – perhaps

Talk to your baby about her favourite toys to promote language development.

practising for later! But by 4 or 5 years old, boys catch up and may be talking their female friends under the table.

In order to utter her first words, your baby's mouth and vocal tract must lengthen and change, which happens around her third month. At that point, it's possible for her to use her tongue, lips, and facial muscles to babble in ways that are surprisingly consistent across dozens of languages.

Once she starts communicating, she quickly learns that babbling and cooing make things happen. For instance, after she squeals and flashes a gummy smile, her mummy cuddles and kisses her; after crying a certain way, she gets fed. Babbling is also your child's way of exercising her tongue and lips to make different vowel-consonant combinations at various decibel levels. Encourage her with lots of funny tongue clicks and raspberries; you're sure to get a smile!

From a very young age, your baby mimics what she hears. In fact, as early as 3 months old, a child's brain can discern differences among several hundred spoken sounds. In one study, 3- to 5-month-old babies watched films of adults making vowel sounds and did so for five minutes a day for three days in a row. Researchers found that even some of the youngest babies tried to copy what they heard and actually did some spot-on imitations.

Did you know?

Psychologists set out to study how using a baby's name and other familiar words helped them better understand language. Results revealed that those as young as 6 months old not only recognized the sound of their own name, but were able to distinguish and recall new words that immediately succeeded it. To broaden your baby's vocabulary, use her name often when talking to her and telling stories, and repeat the same words next to her name. For example, "Lily's bike was shiny and red. Everyone knew that Lily's bike could go really fast."

> " I used to read my baby daughter the reports I had to write for work using funny inflections and entertaining voices as if I were reading a children's book. She got to hear lots of words and I got to proofread my work.
>
> – David, father of two "

How to have fun with it

Talk directly to your baby from day one. Tell him what you're doing such as, "Let's get dressed for Grandma's house" or "That bath water is nice and warm". Repeating words and using inflections to highlight them helps him learn to speak. Yes, at this point you're simply the narrator and may get tired of your own monologue, but research shows that talking and interacting with your baby in this way helps stimulate language and vocabulary development and even lay the groundwork for his reading skills. Studies suggest that infants whose mums chatted with them often learned almost 300 more words by the time they were 2 years old than did those whose mums barely spoke to them.

Most caregivers naturally use what's called "parentese", a sing-song, high-pitched tone of speaking combined with exaggerated facial expressions and short, simple sentences. Unlike baby talk, which consists of made-up words and sounds, parentese means you're elongating and clearly pronouncing consonants and vowels and really enunciating words and repeating them. Experts say that talking this way can actually help you bond with your baby, enhance his language skills by capturing his attention, and help his brain map the sounds he's hearing.

When your baby starts babbling, respond to his sounds as if they were actually words, such as, "Yes, this blanket is soft against your skin, isn't it?" or "I see that you like playing in the bathtub with your duck".

Many parents wonder about the benefits of flash cards or videos that claim to teach babies to talk sooner or dramatically boost their vocabularies. According to several studies, parking your baby in front of a video or computer screen may actually delay language development. Your baby learns best from face-to-face interaction, so get down on the floor with him and start talking. Or play games that include bouncing him on your knee and narrating his "ride".

Singing is another way to expose your little one to words and phrases – and no, you don't have to have a wonderful voice.

In fact, because your voice is familiar, he'll find it comforting and soothing even if you can't hold a tune. Reading aids his language development long before he can understand the plot; in fact, studies show that reading to even the littlest babies stimulates their brains to create new learning pathways and strengthen existing ones.

Besides being educational, lots of kissing, snuggling in your arms, cuddling in your lap, and listening to the loving tone of your voice gives your baby an immense sense of safety and security and reinforces the closeness between the two of you.

learning play

Now you see it, now you don't

What you'll notice

For much of the first year, the only things that exist for your child are right in front of her eyes; out of sight is literally out of mind. That's why your baby doesn't look when she drops her bottle or doesn't remember about a toy you hid under a blanket. When you play peek-a-boo and cover your face with a blanket, she's not sure you'll be there when you remove the blanket; by 9 to 10 months, your child understands the notion of hide-and-seek in a much more sophisticated way. Even if you bury a toy under two or more covers, she will gleefully dig it out.

This new understanding also applies to people. So when you hide behind your hands, she knows where you are even if she can't see your face. Once she understands this, however, your baby may react much more strongly to your disappearance from sight. As a result, you may find that the child who happily let you play "pass the baby" at gatherings with friends and family no longer wants to leave the safety of your arms.

Why it's happening

Though she lived with an out-of-sight-out-of-mind mentality for the first few months of her life, at around 8 months she starts to understand "object permanence", the idea that things or people still exist even though she can't see them. Now she looks for that bottle she dropped because it is around somewhere or lifts up the covers for a game of hide-and-seek. By 10 months, she may be able to identify a toy or other object even when she sees only a tiny piece of it. Separation anxiety – the fear of being separated from Mum or Dad – is also related to object permanence and sets in around 8 or 9 months. Despite your baby's understanding that you haven't vanished, she isn't sure when you're coming back.

How to have fun with it

Hide-and-seek and peek-a-boo help reinforce this concept of object permanence. When your baby is in her cot, crouch down to where she can't see you, then pop up. Repeat this over and over, varying the length of the delay

Lift-the-flap books reinforce the concept of peek-a-boo.

between appearances and she'll respond with visible delight. You can also do this with simple lift-the-flap books or household objects. Take a kitchen towel and cover up a fork while your baby watches. "Where could the fork be?" She'll be thrilled to show you, and happy to play again with a spoon, cup, and other objects whose names you'll be introducing.

When it comes to separations, you can ease anxiety by cuddling and hugging her in the midst of strangers and by letting her warm up slowly in new situations. Or create a "goodbye" ritual that's unique to the two of you that you do without fail each time you leave each other. It could be a little song and a kiss or maybe a special goodbye script delivered by her favourite stuffed animal. Whatever you choose, doing it often will make her feel safe when she's making the transition from your arms to that of a babysitter or other caregiver (and will probably be useful for bigger transitions later in life, like her first day of pre-school or junior school).

loving play

Baby bonding

What you'll notice

Your baby can recognize his parents' faces, voices and smells pretty much from day one. In fact, several studies have demonstrated that the recognition of Mum's voice begins in utero – and as early as the first days after his birth, a newborn will turn toward his mother's voice, even if someone else is holding and speaking to him. He's also busy figuring out how his needs for things like food, love, and comfort are met. This is why he calms down when you hold him – as opposed to someone else – and he can be soothed by the sound of your voice. And by just two months old, he may smile, kick, or wave his arms in the air to show you that he recognizes you.

> " I place my baby on the ground under me while doing push-ups. Every time I go into the down part of the push-up, I give her a kiss. This way we bond and play while I squeeze in a little exercise. "
>
> – Erin, mother of one

By 3 months of age, your baby will be up for longer stretches of time and take an interest in the world around him. At this stage, he'll also enjoy the sound of a rattle or the squeak of a cuddly toy, especially if you're nearby.

Why it's happening

Older relatives may tell you that you can spoil a baby by cuddling him too much or by responding to his cries too quickly. Not true. As you care for your baby, you're helping him develop a sense of security, trust, and self-confidence. Experts in the field say that there's a link between a baby's emotional life and his brain development. There is now a substantial body of research, including actual images of babies' brains, that demonstrates the dramatic impact emotions have on a child's cognitive skills. Language development, problem solving, logic, and the ability to form ideas are directly connected to the kind of emotional nurturing a baby receives. For example, if a baby's basic needs for food and comfort are met, then he can better focus on all the stimulation surrounding him. As he processes this information, he's building new connections among the neurons in his brain. Playing with your baby is one of the best ways to foster an emotional security and help him learn.

How to have fun with it

Even the most basic care-giving tasks – feeding, changing, bathing, and soothing your baby – demonstrate your love. So does snuggling him as you read a book or show him a stuffed animal or play games like "This Little Piggy". But just as babies can soak up your positive emotions, they can sense when you're frazzled. Of course, when you're juggling life with a newborn, stress is par for the course, but it's critical to find ways to nurture yourself and to have fun so you have the emotional resources to draw on when your baby needs you. Make a regular "date" with yourself and, while a friend or spouse watches your little one, take a walk, soak in the bath, or watch your favourite TV show. At first, you may feel guilty taking time away from your child, but being calm and collected is healthy for both of you.

Snuggling as you show your baby a stuffed animal promotes his bond with you.

loving play

Little Miss Personality

What you'll notice

For the first few weeks, when your newborn spends about 60 per cent of her time sleeping, there's not much chance for her personality to emerge. But just a few months into this first year, you'll realize that children have very distinct personalities that come through loud and clear (or calmly and quietly). You may notice that she adores lots of attention and is very extroverted and sociable or that she is shy and more reserved around strangers. She may love lots of noise and activity or may get unhappy when her environment is too overwhelming. And once she is upset, it may take a while for her to calm down – or a distracting toy may do the trick in no time.

An active baby will thrive on the fun of kicking in a vibrating bouncy seat.

> "My first child loved stimulation – he was thrilled by toys with lights and noise. My second child was more sensitive; she preferred just watching what was going on around her.
>
> – Ann, mother of two

Why it's happening

Your child's temperament is inborn, a reflection of her unique genetic makeup. It's surprising to many parents that their offspring's personality may be very different from their own or from an older sibling's. For example, a quiet, introverted mum has an active, "I never want to sleep" baby or a very social, extroverted dad has a slow-to-warm-up baby who gets overwhelmed by too many people. However, just because your child came with this temperament built in doesn't mean you can't affect her behaviour and how she interacts with the world. Learning to work with your child's personality is one of the most important ways you can show your love and understanding.

How to have fun with it

Tailoring play to your baby's temperament is very important, even at this early stage. For example, if you have a baby who's sensitive to a lot of stimulation, make sure your playtime consists mainly of soft singing, reading, and story-telling. On the other hand, if your baby is a social butterfly who thrives on lots of action, she may love to be sung to while she bounces in her bouncy seat. Being passed from one relative to another won't phase her.

Whatever your baby's temperament may be, learn to read her body language. Naturally, you know that crying is a sign that your little one needs something, but less subtle body language provides clues to her needs and feelings. A baby who turns her head or arches her back while playing may be telling you she needs a break. One who tugs her ear or rubs her eyes may be ready for a nap.

Be aware that even when our children are babies, we send messages about the kinds of behaviours we value, many of which relate to our family culture. If you come from a long line of extroverts who hug perfect strangers, you may have a hard time when your little one buries her face in your neck as Grandpa approaches. Don't apologize, just hold her while Grandpa talks to you. Your warm responses to his words will help her feel more comfortable. And no child is totally consistent or predictable. She may surprise you next time and reach out for Grandpa's embrace.

healthy play

The first move

What you'll notice

Gaining control of his head is essential for all the other big moves in your baby's future, which is why it's deemed one of the major milestones of infanthood. During the newborn days, the muscles of the neck and upper back are weak. But at 1 month, your baby may be able to lift his head momentarily, and by 3 to 5 months, he'll be able to hold it up pretty steadily.

Another major baby move? Turning over. He'll probably roll from front to back at 3 to 5 months, but may not master the more challenging back-to-front flip until he's closer to 5 to 6 months.

Anywhere between the 6- and 9-month mark, your baby will probably sit unsupported. Watch his delight at this new view of his surroundings as he points to and reaches for objects that he couldn't see when he was flat on his back. Just don't get too comfortable with this stage. In a matter of months, this desire will propel him towards the next milestone: crawling. He may start with the "army" or "crab" crawl, using his arms and scooting along the floor on his stomach.

For his next trick, your child will learn to go from lying down to sitting up – without any help from you. This often happens as his first birthday approaches, and around the same time he's likely to pull himself to standing and even take a few steps while holding onto furniture or someone's hand.

Why it's happening

This year your baby is getting sturdier, even if his developing muscles are buried under layers of yummy baby fat. Every muscle in his tiny body is developing and his coordination is improving: his stronger neck and upper back muscles help him lift his head; arm muscles help him do a push up; and lower back muscles help him sit. More leg strength is just what he needs to crawl, stand, and cruise.

Curiosity about his surroundings is another reason why he's driven to get moving. He pushes up to improve his view, rolls over to get closer to you, and scoots along on his stomach or pulls himself to standing to retrieve an out-of-reach toy.

How to have fun with it

For babies 1 month and older, tummy time during the day (but never for sleep) helps develop head control. Place your child on a blanket or play mat and lie in front of him with enticing, colourful toys or objects. Once

A mirror inspires your baby to turn his head and work his neck muscles.

he gains more head control, try holding a toy higher than his sightline to encourage him to look up. A baby mirror, either on the floor or attached to the side of his cot, also makes him raise and turn his head to look at himself.

As early as 2 months old, your baby can be propped up with cushions or placed in a swing to help strengthen those all-important head and back muscles. Entertain him with toys, songs, or books so he enjoys sitting. Just make sure you're within reach in case he starts to topple over and don't prop him up any longer than an hour at a time. If he seems fussy, he may need a break even sooner.

Help strengthen your baby's muscles by showing him how to move different body parts. While he's lying down, gently move his legs as if he's cycling or doing a flutter kick and lift his arms up and down over his head. Do some baby sit ups by holding your baby's hands while he's lying on his back and gently pulling him up to a sitting position. Repeat a few times in order to strengthen those tiny neck and upper back muscles. Encourage rolling or crawling by

Playing it safe

Though it's fun to play with your baby when he can sit up, be sure not to put baby seats or car seats on countertops or other raised surfaces. And never leave a seated baby unattended.

placing an interesting colourful object close enough for him to see, but not touch. If your baby's legs seem strong enough around the age of 10 or 11 months, hold his hands and take him for a stroll – great preparation for walking on his own.

healthy play

Getting a grip

What you'll notice

Reach out and touch someone – or something. That's what your baby's trying to do as early as 12 weeks of age. He'll try to grip and grasp things like your finger, a rattle, even your hair. His curious hands will continue their explorations over the next few months, and soon his mouth will become another tool for discovery. At first he'll hold things in the palm of his hand using all his fingers, but as early as 8 months, he'll be able to use a pincer grip, picking up smaller objects with his thumb and index finger. Nine or ten months into this first year, you may wonder if you're living with a baby or a marching band. That's because banging is a big hit with babies and he'll clank together whatever he can from toy bricks to pot lids to his own two hands. Soon, he'll have mastered the ability to transfer an object from one hand to the other and to turn it over.

A rattle helps your baby to hone grasping skills.

Why it's happening

Almost daily your baby's muscles are strengthening, his coordination and balance are improving and nerve pathways needed for movement are being laid down in his brain. The result is better small and large muscle control. Grabbing and gripping are your baby's ways of "seeing" the world. In fact, in a study of infants' tactile memory, researchers filmed 12-month-olds as they played with unfamiliar and familiar objects first in a lit room and then with the lights turned off. In both situations, the babies spent more time handling unfamiliar objects – using primarily their hands and mouths to get to know these novel toys.

You may not love the noise created by your baby's banging, but it's music to his ears – another way for him to delve into his environment. He's learned to hold an object in each hand simultaneously and realizes that he can use these things in a way that creates sound. (Provide the "Boom! Boom!" sound effects to add to the fun.) Just make sure to steer him toward safe noisemakers – plastic rattles, bricks, or toy instruments – and away from potentially dangerous things such as glass tables or breakable objects.

How to have fun with it

A baby as young as 3 months will like lying under a mobile or dangling toy. He'll probably try swiping it with his little fist – a motion that is his first step towards the more complicated task of actually reaching for something. If the toy moves or makes a sound when he hits it, that will encourage him to keep aiming for it. Repeating this will refine his reaching skills.

Encourage your child's fine motor skills by letting him hold toys of different shapes and sizes and giving him a demonstration on how they work. For example, shake the rattle so he can hear what's inside or, when he's a little older, show him how to push the button on a toy car to hear its horn beep.

Stimulate his sense of touch by exposing him to a variety of textures like the fur of a stuffed (or real) dog, a piece of wood, fabrics like satin, corduroy, and denim, carpet, and even Daddy's stubbly chin. Label each sensation as you run his hand over the surface: "Wow! Daddy's beard feels scratchy". Reading touch-and-feel books can have the same impact – just don't be surprised if he spends as much time mouthing the pages as he does staring at the pictures.

Homemade fun

Is taking things out of Mum's purse your baby's favourite game? If so, give him a spare handbag filled with baby-safe items like an old wallet, glasses case, plastic key ring, even a few small stuffed animals.

one-year-olds
The Age of Discovery

* * *

play milestones for this year

STACK
bricks or
plastic cups

TALK
with dolls,
stuffed animals,
and puppets

FILL
containers,
then empty
them out

IMITATE
grown-up
behaviour

SORT
toys by shape

IDENTIFY
"boy" and "girl"
toys

WALK
while
pulling a toy

The Age of Discovery

For many parents, the weeks following that first birthday cake are as miraculous as those hazy days after the birth. You knew your baby had plenty of personality, but suddenly, a whole new side of him steps out. In fact, the transformation from infant to little person is enough to take your breath away. You ask yourself, "Who is this amazing child?"

Of course, the big news this year is that your little wonder will take his first steps. This new, upright view of the world, combined with his increased physical ability and natural curiosity, means he's no longer content to simply stare at things. Your child is moving – literally – into a phase of exploratory play that opens up an exciting array of new toys.

Thanks to toddlers' stronger fine motor skills, four distinct types of play begin to capture their attention, whether they live in the Amazonian rain forest or central London. They want to stack things, like bricks; nest things, like plastic cups; gather and empty things, like containers of water; and manipulate small objects.

Your toddler's brain is also working overtime. One monumental breakthrough, which occurs around the first birthday, is the recognition that he is his own person, separate from Mum or Dad. By 18 months, he will recognize himself in a mirror, use his own name, and even point to himself in family photos. Games such as, "Where's Christopher?" are likely to be a huge hit.

As intoxicating as all this autonomy is, it's also a little scary, which is why separation and stranger anxiety peak at around 15 months. At this stage, about 60 per cent of children latch onto the most important toy of their lives – a security object. Whether it's called a lovey, a blankie, or just plain Teddy, this toy comforts children when they're frightened or when they're making the transition from wakefulness to sleep.

"I have an impact on the world!" That's the realization your toddler makes as he grasps the notion of cause and effect and why he whacks his cup on the table over and over (and over) again. Mastering these concepts requires and enhances another brand-new skill: memory. By 18 months or so, he remembers where the triangle goes in the shape sorter, and doesn't have to test every corner. And these are long-term memories. Researchers at Harvard University discovered that children between the ages of 21 to 28 months could recall a sequence of events they had last seen four months prior.

Your toddler is also busy expanding his vocabulary. Whatever he says these days, whether it's "Down!" "Mine!" or the increasingly popular "No!" he's likely to say it with a conviction that's brand new. And even if he isn't using many words, he is beginning to understand a lot more.

One of the top cognitive breakthroughs at this time is your child's ability to imitate you – chatting on a toy mobile phone, for example, and using his imagination very differently. He understands that something pretend – a doll – stands for something real – a baby. At some point, between 18 and 21 months, a child who had only used a doll to bang on the cot rail is now feeding it pretend waffles and kissing it good night.

learning play

Yakkety yak!

ga ga

da

ba

da

ga

ma

What you'll notice

Most toddlers say a handful of words by their first birthday, and continue adding a few here and there on a daily basis. Neuroscientists have concluded that 50 is the magic number: once your toddler has mastered roughly four dozen words, a language explosion begins, and he'll constantly surprise you with new adorably pronounced (or mispronounced) words. Most children say more than 150 by the time they are 20 months old; 300 or so by their second birthday. But if mum's the word at your house, don't panic. Kids develop the gift of the gab at their own pace. In fact, an estimated 10 per cent of toddlers talk later than do their peers. (Of course, if you're concerned about this or any other milestone, talk to your doctor.)

As the new words come tumbling out, it's fun to watch children discover their own linguistic logic. Most toddlers, for instance,

Use puppets to have a pretend conversation with your child, building her vocabulary.

over-generalize. "Doggie", once reserved for the dachshund next door, may now refer to any four-legged animal. And if "Go!" was once a word that meant "buggy", he may now apply it to a car, bus – even his jacket. Next come two-word phrases: "More sing" or "Me ball".

Your 1-year-old's listening skills are developing rapidly, too. He can look and listen at the same time and do so longer than before. In the months leading up to his second birthday, he'll be able to point at pictures and objects when you ask, follow basic instructions, and – brace yourself – repeat words he hears in your conversations.

Did you know?

To understand the link between the listening and speaking areas of the brain in newborns, in 6-month-olds, and in 1-year-olds, researchers at the University of Washington's Institute for Brain and Learning Sciences used special equipment to monitor their brains. All three age groups showed activity in the area of the brain linked to listening and understanding speech. But only the 1-year-olds showed simultaneous activity in the areas that hear language and produce language.

Why it's happening

Toddlers turn talkative because of a major spurt in brain development. Language activity shifts from a large, unspecialized area of the cerebral cortex to the temporal-parietal areas, which include distinct brain centres that process comprehension (what words mean) and grammar (how words go together). As early as 16 months, children put their two-word sentences in proper grammatical order, most of the time ("All gone!" "See kitty!"). The more he practises, the more sophisticated the wiring in this section of the brain becomes, laying the groundwork for a vocabulary bonanza.

How to have fun with it

The more you talk, the richer your toddler's vocabulary will eventually be, so create a language-rich environment. Sing, recite nursery rhymes (he'll enjoy the rhythm and repetition of familiar words), and talk about objects as you play. Ask plenty of questions, even if the answers only come in gesture form. Dialogue-filled games teach your future chatterbox that conversations consist of a certain pacing and give-and-take. Place a puppet (or sock) on each of your hands – or grab a couple of stuffed animals or little figures – and make them talk to each other in two different voices. Give him a puppet or stuffed animal, too, but don't force him to do anything with it. It may be enough for him to take in the show you put on.

Read with your child every day, letting him choose the stories and turn the pages. Say things like, "Can you point to the apple?" or "Where's the cow?" an exercise that lets him show off how many words he understands even if he can't actually say them. Your delighted response to his correct answers will boost his desire to chat even more.

learning play

Play it again

What you'll notice

"More! More!" is probably a familiar refrain coming from your toddler when you finish his favourite book, song, or game. Though reading *Where's Spot?* five times or singing endless verses of "Twinkle, Twinkle, Little Star" may drive you barmy, these encore performances are actually an important learning tool.

Repetition also takes centre stage during your child's solo playtime. He repeatedly lifts and lowers the boot on his favourite car, hammers the same toy nail, or opens and closes a kitchen drawer. At first, these actions may be random – he accidentally drops his beaker or hits a spoon on the tabletop. But when he sees you leap up to retrieve the cup or realizes that the spoon makes a loud noise, he's intrigued. "Will it happen again?" he thinks. "And again?

Playing it safe

Children this age put many objects in their mouths as another way to explore them. In addition to paying very close attention to anything that could be a choking hazard, be wary of objects and toys that may contain lead paint, which actually tastes sweet. And keep up to date on product recalls by visiting the Trading Standards Central website at www.tradingstandards.gov.uk.

Let's see." He investigates by duplicating his initial action and after testing his hypotheses several times, he learns that some things in life are predictable – a notion that can be comforting and provide an amazing feeling of power.

Why it's happening

All this repetition helps your extremely curious toddler uncover how things work and strengthens his problem-solving skills. It also imprints newly acquired abilities into his growing brain. Like a mini Einstein, your child is studying his environment and experimenting, which allows him to grasp intriguing concepts like up, down, open, closed, solid, hollow, soft, and rough. It also introduces the notion of causality and the thrilling idea that his actions affect the world around him.

While you may question the entertainment value of the sixth reading of *Peace at Last*, your little one doesn't. Initially, he's not sure if you'll say the same words as before, but with each time, he discovers that you will. Soon enough, your child learns the words to that favourite story or song and, even if he can't recite them, knowing what comes next is all at once exciting, comforting, rewarding, and a huge confidence booster. It also helps him figure out the order of events, and this extends beyond playtime. For example, he begins to understand that certain activities happen in a predictable order: pyjamas follow bathtime or the sight of the dog's lead means he's going out for a walk.

How to have fun with it

Though the same book or song makes you feel like a broken record and your child making the same noise or doing the same action over and over can get on your nerves, try not to get frustrated or refuse your child's request. (If you can't stand another reading of the same book, maybe another adult in the house can step in.) Provide plenty of toys that let your child practise cause and effect, like books with flaps or toys with buttons and levers. Everyday items can also please your pint-size experimenter: plastic containers with lids or even a glasses case that opens and closes. He may also have a hard time resisting the urge to open and bang shut a door or a drawer, even after you've told him "No!" At this age, he has very little impulse control and may need your help finding something equally entertaining, but safer and less annoying, with which to engage. The good news is that his understanding of cause and effect enables him to begin to learn

which behaviours are unacceptable. Keep your discipline simple and state your reasons clearly and plainly: "When you hit, you can't play with the toys."

Also, thanks to this repetition, his fine motor skills are developing and this means that an array of creative play options are on his horizon: drawing with big crayons, handling chunky puzzle pieces, rolling modelling dough, and holding books so he can "read" to himself.

A Jack-in-the-Box reinforces the thrilling idea that actions can have effects.

learning play

The land of make-believe

What you'll notice

Around the 18-month mark, you may find that you've got a Mini-Me in tow. At this age children begin using items, such as a toy phone as a phone (rather than a drumstick to the ear) or a baby doll as a child. In doing so, they also start copying how the adults around them act: they type on a pretend computer, cook in a play kitchen, or don Dad's sunglasses. Your toddler's imagination comes to life, and so does the world around her, as her stuffed toys take on personalities or as she transforms a cardboard shoe box into a stove or fast car.

"When I want to get my son to help me clean up, I'll tell him to pretend that he's a forklift truck picking up blocks and dumping them in a box or a vacuum making a loud "vroom-vroom" noise as he works."

— Julie, mother of three

Why it's happening

Your toddler chatting on her faux phone or hosting a pretend tea party is more than adorable. With her new memory skills, she can mimic adult behaviour because she remembers how Dad uses his laptop or how Mum carries her handbag. This role playing teaches your child about social interactions and behaviour. It may also reveal concerns or anxieties. For example, a child who's anxious about having a new babysitter may act this out by having her stuffed animal or doll experience the same thing. Pretend play also helps her develop much-needed skills. Studies show children with highly developed fantasy lives not only have better concentration and self-control; they also think of more creative ways to solve problems.

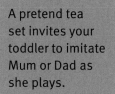

A pretend tea set invites your toddler to imitate Mum or Dad as she plays.

How to have fun with it

Basic household items – like empty cereal boxes, paper towel rolls, and your old clothes – provide great fodder for make-believe. The same goes for toys: dolls, doll prams, bottles, unbreakable tea sets, tool benches, and child-sized role-playing props like doctor's kits, purses, tea sets, and tool kits. When your child invites you into her fantasy world, resist the urge to direct the action. This is your child's show and letting her run it encourages creativity and boosts her imagination.

Providing your child with a multitude of real-world experiences will also help develop her fantasy play. For example, if you take her to the zoo and introduce her to a real, live giraffe, her stuffed giraffe at home will become the vehicle for an even greater level of imaginative play.

Whatever path her imagination may take, your attitude will affect its course. Allow time for her to pretend without worrying about a mess or an end goal. And if she doesn't feel like pretending at a particular moment, don't force it. Follow her lead.

loving play

Getting to know me

What you'll notice

Though hints of a baby's personality emerge around 4 months, by now you have a real sense of his or her temperament. Some of the earliest researchers in this field, doctors Alexander Thomas and Stella Chase, noticed four common temperaments and labelled them easy, slow-to-warm-up, difficult, and active. Naturally, we're all unique and don't fit neatly into four simple categories, but this breakdown does provide a basic understanding of your little one's personality. Becoming aware of his temperament can help you determine the best play to bring out his strengths and help him manage challenging situations.

Sorting toys help toddlers tolerate frustration – an important skill.

Children with an easy temperament have no problem transitioning smoothly from one activity to the next. These toddlers are typically in a good mood and have moderate – rather than intense – emotions.

Those in the slow-to-warm-up group need time to adapt to unfamiliar situations, cautiously observing from a distance before participating. Change and transitions are hard for these children, who are often considered shy or anxious and prefer mellower activities.

The toddler with the difficult temperament is sensitive to too much stimulation or change in routine. He can be hard to please and benefits from being talked through tough transitions ("I know it's hard to leave the playground") and for being accepted for who he is.

Lastly, there's the active category. Rather than walk or crawl, these children have energy to burn and their impulsive and fearless natures may make it more difficult to keep them safe.

Why it's happening

Your child's temperament is inborn, so it's been part of him since his early days. However, just because your child came pre-wired with his unique temperament doesn't mean you can't affect his behaviour and how he interacts with the world. Learning to work with, not against, your child's personality is one of the most important ways to show your love and understanding. It also makes life with a toddler a lot easier!

Homemade fun

Choose books to read that match your baby's temperament. Wild characters will suit active children, while those about new situations, like moving or going to the doctor, will appeal to the slow-to-warm-up child.

How to have fun with it

Playdates, playgroups, and other social activities are a blast for your easy-going child. Because he's so laid back and doesn't make much of a fuss, it's natural to assume he's okay with any game or toy or with playing by himself. And though he may be, it's important to add variety and join him at times so that he's exposed to a variety of toys and forms of play.

The slow-to-warm-up child is more likely to feel comfortable with familiar toys, games, books, and songs. Help him ease into a new situation by saying, "Look, Colin has the same bricks that you do", or by getting new people to use a favourite toy to connect with him. Give him plenty of warning before trying something new.

Since those in the difficult group are easily over-stimulated, keep toys to a minimum. If you notice him frustrated with a particular toy, don't parachute in to "save" him. Let him begin to build the muscles necessary to tolerate a little frustration, but if he gets upset, hold him for a few minutes or rub his back gently.

Give your Energizer Bunny toddler room to roam, and make sure he's well supervised. To help these easily distracted children stay focused, rotate toys and games a few at a time.

loving play

Boy meets girl

What you'll notice

With children's blossoming sense of autonomy comes lots of ways to define themselves: preferring baths on the cool side, liking orange juice better than apple, and hating sweaters that itch. Believe it or not, they're also figuring out that girls are different from boys, or vice versa.

To test the precise age at which this happens, researchers from Pennsylvania State University experimented by giving a group of toddlers dolls dressed as boys and girls. At 18 months, children don't seem to notice, and treat the male dolls just the same as the female ones. But between 18 and 22 months, there is a sharp increase in the children's awareness. It's not that they prefer one sex to another, researchers say – but they are starting to sort them out.

Why it's happening

It's easy to believe a toddler's perceptions of what's masculine or feminine are inborn rather than learned. But experts say they're getting gender stereotypes from TV, advertising, and the people around them. Psychologists at Brigham Young University have found that children between 18 and 24 months will stare longer at "gender inconsistent" photos, such as a man doing housework. And a team of Canadian researchers have shown that by 18 months, toddlers already associate images like bears and hammers with men, and things like cats and dresses with women. When Dad does his fair share of the housework and then encourages his son to use his toy broom and dustpan, he's not only contributing to the needs of the family, he's also modelling a powerful image for his son or daughter.

Whether through gestures or words, parents and caregivers communicate messages about gender that influence the ways in which children develop. Girls, for example, are often slightly more verbal than boys, and their ability to talk earlier may have some basis in biology. But linguists now believe that that the gift of the gab happens because parents tend to talk to girls differently, using more words to describe feelings, for example, and asking more questions. With boys, parents are more likely to use short, imperative sentences.

Gender-neutral toys like balls will encourage toddlers to be open-minded in their play.

How to have fun with it

Create a gender-neutral toy box. Despite your toddler's growing awareness of gender, both sexes are still equally attracted to all toys. Friends and family members will probably shower your little girl with dolls and princess gear; just make sure she's got some trucks and balls, too. Vice versa for your son. If he hugs a doll lovingly, say, "You're going to be such a wonderful Daddy", and if your daughter grabs a ball, encourage her to "Throw it hard!"

Did you know?

Researchers at the University of Kansas studied 40 pairs of toddlers and their parents and found that when playing with typical boy toys like trucks, parents used more animated sounds and had fewer verbal interactions. When playing with stereotypical girl toys like dolls, parents had more verbal communication and sat physically closer to their children. Next time you play with boy toys, try talking about the adventures the toys are having in addition to providing sound effects.

healthy play

Stepping out

What you'll notice

Even if your toddler isn't walking yet, she's constantly on the move. By 12 months, she can stand without support, and around 14 months, most children are squatting while playing, bending, and climbing stairs and slides, as well as scaling chairs and piles of pillows. Crawling, creeping, and cruising quickly turn into walking, usually by about 13 to 15 months.

Soon, your ball of energy will start running and barrelling down corridors. At first, she'll do so while focusing her gaze on the ground in front of her and she may stumble when she has to change direction. But by the end of this year, that cute stiff-legged gait will turn into a steadier stride, using a basic heel-toe motion just like adults. She'll probably run in a straight line, step to the side, and even walk backwards. And while she won't be able to walk up stairs alternating feet just yet, she will be able to go up and down the steps unaided – but not unsupervised.

Playing it safe

Your child is making like a monkey and the playground is a great place to practise her climbing skills – with you in close proximity. Just make sure the one you choose is age-appropriate, not filled with equipment made for older children, with them barrelling around (and potentially into) your little one.

Why it's happening

Your toddler is increasingly aware of the huge world around her and naturally curious. Right now, her only goal is to explore it using her own steam. In the flurry of perpetual motion, walking certainly gets most of her attention; after all, that's why we call them toddlers. But every day, she's challenging herself to try a variety of skills and learns by engaging with the world. If she sees a toy she wants on a high shelf, she may drag a chair over and climb it. She may swing on the curtains like Tarzan just to see how it feels. She may spend 20 minutes tunnelling under your bed – and that's all before her morning nap.

This new mobility and the freedom to explore certainly boosts your child's muscle strength, but it also has a positive impact on her emotional and cognitive development. To your toddler, there's no bigger confidence booster than being able to walk towards and pick up what she wants all by herself.

How to have fun with it

Keep a variety of balls around the house. While many children won't actually be able to kick until the end of this year, most will find some way to propel a ball with their feet. And watch her throwing skills develop. Early on, she'll use a stiff-armed, underhanded toss. But soon, she'll figure out that she can make the ball go further by bending her elbow.

Cushions and pillows are a toddler's best friend. Turn the living room into an obstacle course, complete with sofa-cushion bridges and white-sheet tunnels. A hula hoop to step in and out of will add to the challenge.

These improved gross motor skills combined with better hand-eye coordination make pull toys with strings and push toys with handles favourites among the toddler set.

Catch her if you can! A toddler's ability to run means a game of tag is in your immediate future. The thrill of the chase is more than fun; it lets her learn about boundaries and reaffirms the fact that even though she can move away from you, you're close by. If you're too exhausted for the chase, simply blow some bubbles and let her run after them.

Push toys help one-year-olds develop their walking skills.

two-year-olds

Independence Days

* * *

play milestones for this year

PLAY SOLO
for longer stretches of time

IMPROVE MEMORY
with matching games

PARALLEL PLAY
with peers

FOLLOW THE RULES
for easy games

PRETEND
with baby dolls, animals, and playsets

MANAGE SELF-CARE TASKS
like brushing teeth

PEDAL
a tricycle

Independence Days

The year between your child's second and third birthdays is rife with contradictions. On the one hand, your toddler seems like a baby: he's probably still in nappies; clings to his security blanket; and won't give up his dummy. On the other hand, he walks and talks like a real little person, communicating most of his needs, and listening better (when he wants to). He may look and act quite capable – and he is compared to last year – and yet there's so much that he wants to do but can't. He can run, jump, and climb, but he's not always steady and can't reach as far or as high as he'd like. By the middle of this year, it is likely that he'll know as many as 900 words and use longer sentences, yet he often lacks the vocabulary to describe his needs or emotions.

Life is exciting, but it can also be overwhelming and extremely frustrating for even the most easy-going 2-year-old. Whether you agree that this year is aptly called "the terrible twos" or you sail through with few challenges, you can anticipate more of a roller-coaster ride than you've faced in the past. Though it's not easy, look at the bright side: it's a sign that your child is continuing to evolve into her own unique person.

All these new abilities and an insatiable hunger to explore his environment require Mum and Dad to put more limits on what he can do. According to research, 2-year-olds are told "No!" every 9 minutes. And he's not the only one feeling the pain. One moment your sweet-tempered child seems independent and capable; the next he flings herself on the floor, kicking and screaming.

No matter what your toddler's temperament may be, his battle cry for this year is almost guaranteed to be "I do it!" And he's not asking you if he can, he's telling you that he will. Another well-worn phrase of the toddler set – "Mine!" – reflects the fact that sharing is not his strongpoint; he's unable to understand that not everything is his. But the dominant word in his vocabulary will probably be "No!" said loud and clear and often – even at times when he really means "Yes". "No!" is the one push-back expression that helps him maintain a sense of independence and control over a world that can feel very big and overwhelming.

Despite the rough patches, there's also a lot to relish. This year your toddler will take his first steps into the world of friendships. On the other end of the play spectrum, he is also happy and able to entertain himself. Thanks to his new abilities, your time together guarantees plenty of fun and wonder and laughs. And what's better than the sound of a toddler's belly laugh? Not surprisingly, these years are often the time when dads become more involved in their children's lives. Dramatic advances in your child's physical abilities mean you can kick a ball around with him in the garden, jog behind him on his new tricycle, or just go on walks together. He can even follow simple rules, so basic board and card games can be added to his play repertoire.

learning play

Going solo

What you'll notice

Many children this age are great at entertaining themselves. In fact, you'll be dazzled as your toddler turns anything from a cardboard box to a shopping bag into a spaceship or a car. One day that empty cereal container is a drum; the next day it's his puppy. His make-believe skills promise longer stretches of solo time spent "fixing" with plastic tools or taking his favourite stuffed animals for a ride. His ability to animate his play with different voices and a storyline speak to a host of cognitive changes, including a vocabulary that's growing at a rate of approximately five new words per day. Unlike his baby years, when books were primarily enjoyed as objects, the content of his favourite books will draw him to them again and again. Though he can't read, he may sit and turn the pages, reciting familiar stories or making up his own.

Why it's happening

Your child's improved fine and gross motor skills make him better able to manipulate things and explore on his own. He no longer needs you to take the lid off the puzzle box, can open and close drawers and cupboards, and can don his cowboy hat or fireman's jacket by himself.

One of the most important cognitive developments during this year is the understanding that one object can symbolize another: the plush dog represents a real dog, the shoe-box the dog's bed. In a related development, he realizes that he can make believe that he's someone else – say, Daddy, Mummy, or his doctor – without actually being that person. It's also at this age that he starts noticing differences in people's appearances. Fuelled by his more active imagination, these advances open up an array of make-believe worlds for him to jump into. And with more than two years' experience, he's able to bring a wealth of information into his pretend scenarios. At the same time, as he steps into

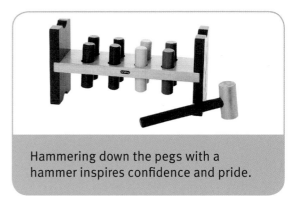

Hammering down the pegs with a hammer inspires confidence and pride.

the shoes of those around him, he's beginning to make sense of his world and the important players in it. When he packs a shopping bag with construction paper and tells you loudly, "I go. No cry, baby", he's working through challenges – like separations – in ways that help him cope when it's time for Mummy and Daddy to leave for work.

More advanced problem-solving and thinking skills also mean that he doesn't need you by his side to guide his play. He knows how to test all sides of a puzzle piece to see if it fits or to stack the bricks differently if they won't stay upright. And even when he can't solve a problem immediately, he's exercising a trait that he didn't have last year and that will serve him well in the future: persistence.

> " I was really surprised when my toddler suddenly rediscovered his baby toys and used them in new ways: a shape sorter became a cash register and old bath toys became his favourite pretend pets. "
>
> – Samantha, mother of three

How to have fun with it

Providing ample time for unstructured play will encourage your child to entertain himself. Not only will he learn a lot from it, but you'll be thankful later on when you don't have a 5-year-old constantly asking, "What should I do now?" In the beginning, you may have to demonstrate how to play with a toy or game, but soon enough, he'll take over. In fact, leave him alone and he'll probably transform that game into something totally different. Or give him a jumping off point by saying, "I wonder what you can make out of this egg carton?" or "Why don't you bring your dog to the park?" After that, stand back, and let him show you what the experts know to be true: children learn best from the games they create themselves.

When your toddler hits a bump in the road and you see her struggling with a puzzle or toy, resist the urge to rescue. Helicopter parents, who hover and then swoop in to "save" the day, actually do their children a big disservice. Unless your child is clearly about to lose it completely, it's far better for her to problem solve, to engage in trial and error, and to muscle through the frustration she experiences as she tries to wrestle her baby doll into a dress. In fact, several research studies have shown that young children who learn to persist with a task and to overcome obstacles grow up to be more self-confident, patient, and successful. One thing is certain: when she holds up that doll – dressed and ready – her sense of pride and self-esteem will be written all over her beaming face.

To encourage solo play, stock up on the right tools. These tend to be "open-ended" toys – those that spark creativity on your child's part rather than electronic or motorized toys where the push of a button does the work. A box filled with paper towel inner tubes, egg cartons, shoe boxes, empty cereal boxes, wrapping paper, old magazines, plastic containers, and fabric scraps will inspire plenty of fun. Dress-up clothes, an old briefcase, a cobbler's bench, tool and tea sets, and miniature brooms or

Homemade fun

Encourage your child to play solo by setting up his own "office" at the kitchen counter or coffee table. Give him some pens, notepads, file folders, a calculator, old phone, and extra keyboard (if you have one). He'll be engrossed in his own play while you make dinner or pay bills.

rakes are all great props for pretend play, while plastic, wood, or plush versions of his favourite characters and animals, puppets, and dolls will help populate his world. An art box with crayons, paper, colouring books, glue sticks, and stickers can be a big hit at this age. No matter what kind of play your toddler seems to enjoy, keep just a few toys and props out at a time, rotating them every other week. This way your child won't get overwhelmed by too many options and his old toys will seem new again when they reappear a few weeks later.

Of course some children are better than others when it comes to playing alone. Toddlers who are highly active and social are going to have a hard time sitting quietly by themselves. Some research indicates that firstborns may be less able to handle solo play because they're used to caregivers acting as playmates. And some parents find it hard to step back and refrain from directing or interfering, especially when their children are frustrated.

learning play

Sooner and later

What you'll notice

Last year or even early this year, if you told your child to wait "just a minute" for her juice, she may have burst into tears or immediately repeated her request. But by the middle to the end of this third year, given the same response, she may say, "Okay", and wait a few minutes for her juice. Following directions comes more easily, as do transitions from one activity to another. She not only understands what you're saying better, but you may also understand and be able to anticipate her needs better.

Why it's happening

Of course, your 2-year-old can't tell the time or know exactly what a minute is, but experience has taught her that this expression means that she will get what she wants soon. In addition, she has a greater understanding of the concept of "later" and can grasp the fact that certain events occur in a predictable sequence. Her improved memory and longer attention span make it easier for her to exercise more patience.

Toddlers' developing sense of time is also enhanced by the routines that give structure to their day. For example, your 2-year-old knows that when Mum leaves for work, it's the morning,

> **"** I gave my daughter an active role in helping me get out of the door in the morning. It was her job to bring me my bag, and then to close the door behind me. This gave her the sense of control she needed to cope with my leaving for work. **"**
>
> – Hayley, mother of two

and that bathtime means it's night and close to bedtime. Daily routines not only make concepts of time tangible, they provide a feeling of comfort: the world feels more manageable and safe when you know what's going to happen next.

Her language development also reflects her newfound grasp of time. When she exclaims, "I goed" or, "I hided", she's showing a more sophisticated understanding of how the English language works and of how the suffix "ed" can be used to describe events in the past.

How to have fun with it

Now that your child understands that certain events follow certain sequences, you can provide her with a sense of control. When the

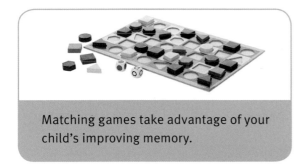

Matching games take advantage of your child's improving memory.

time to leave the playground approaches, for example, tell your child what to expect: "We'll leave the playground after you go down the slide two more times." You can also channel her desire to exert some control over her environment to get her to tidy up or to eat her veggies. At this age, she'll understand what you mean when you say, "As soon as you've put away your toys, we can fingerpaint."

When you play together, your toddler's ability to understand and to follow simple directions will make it possible for her to enjoy board games like Candy Land, and her amazing memory may make her a champ at card games like Concentration.

A wonderful way to boost your child's language skills is to ask open-ended questions like "Where is your pussy-cat going today?" When she does respond with those endearing malapropisms and grammatical mistakes, resist the urge to correct her (which she won't understand anyway); instead, answer her using proper English. For example, when she says, "I hided in the cupboard" respond with "Wow! You hid in the cupboard? For how long?"

loving play

You've got a friend in me

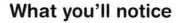

What you'll notice

Just months ago, your child loved looking at babies' faces in books. But, in person, she engaged in what's called "parallel play" – sitting near another child, but not interacting. All that changes this year as she begins to interact with her peers – often called collaborative or cooperative play – and to form friendships. In the beginning, she may simply observe other children rather than play with them (and she'll probably be especially enthralled by those who are older). But as the year progresses, she'll go from the sidelines to the middle of the action – a shift that promises new adventures and challenges.

Why it's happening

For a few years now, your toddler's been learning about the world by watching you and other adults. But at this stage, she makes the thrilling realization that she's her own person, separate from Mum and Dad, and that the world is actually filled with other people besides her immediate family. Additionally, her enhanced cognitive and physical abilities mean that she can run, climb, and pretend better – all of which make her an excellent playmate.

Friendships help your child understand social rules and behaviours, like turn-taking, manners, sharing, and compromise. Playing with a friend also teaches her to express her emotions, communicate better, and take other people's feelings into consideration. By 24 months, your toddler is well aware that not everyone shares her thoughts and feelings – a huge cognitive leap that has a big impact on the way she plays with others.

How to have fun with it

Pull out the calendar and pencil in those playdates. Arrange them for a time when your child is fresh – not right before or instead of her naptime – and invite just one or two friends since too many children can be overwhelming (for both of you). Also, keep the date short; about half an hour to an hour is long enough for this age group. Even a 2-year-old can follow simple rules, so teach your child games that she can play with her friends.

When it comes to sharing, don't get upset when your child asserts, "Mine!" loudly and often. Two-year-olds the world over resent other children moving in on their toys – even the ones they may not particularly covet. Part of your child's unwillingness to share is a need

Did you know?

Studies show that children who have at least one close friend before a sibling is born have better relationships with their new brother or sister. Researchers followed children from the time they were toddlers until they graduated from sixth form and found that this impact was long term. So encourage a friendship if you see one developing – especially if a sibling is on the horizon!

to control her environment. She also doesn't realize her friend is just borrowing a toy – not taking it home. If mid-playdate your child has a death-grip on a specific object, tell her that you'll put it away so no one can play with it. Or offer a distracting swap: "Wow! Look at this cool car. David can play with the train set while you race the car." Also, if your child is squabbling more than usual or has a meltdown mid-playdate, it may be that she's too tired to play – even though she won't tell you that – so you should cut the date short.

Direct your child and her friend towards toys that you have lots of, like crayons, play dough, or dressing-up clothes. When she does share, praise her on the spot and when her pal leaves. And don't worry about your child's hoarding instinct. By her third birthday, she'll realize that not every item in the world is hers.

A ride-on toy that fits two is perfect for playmates.

loving play

The moody twos

What you'll notice

This age isn't called the "terrible twos" for nothing. Though not all children go through it (or some may instead experience the terrible threes), shortly after his second birthday your child may be more emotional and temperamental than ever. He may throw tantrums when he doesn't get what he wants, or break down and cry when he's overwhelmed or frustrated. Something as minor as a broken biscuit can set him off, and when you offer him a new one, he is likely to scream "No!" even if he actually wants it.

Why it's happening

Your 2-year-old's desire to do certain things – like climb to the top rung of the jungle gym or tell you what he needs – often lags behind the development of the requisite physical, mental, and language skills. Sometimes the emotions he experiences, but doesn't have the words for, can be unfamiliar and overwhelming. Not being able to express himself can be extremely frustrating (it's a bit like being in a foreign country and not knowing the language). As a result, he feels that his only option is to scream, cry, or hurl that piece of wooden fruit across the room. Also difficult is the realization that as much as he'd like to control the world around him, he can't. Grown-ups still direct much of his life and tell him what to do – or more likely, what not to do – and all those instructions and "nos" stifle his sense of autonomy. The result can be mood swings and temper tantrums.

Another source of frustration for both of you is that you may overestimate his capabilities. After all, since he's made such huge strides in some areas and seems like this real little person – you may assume that he understands what you're saying better and can control his behaviour more than he actually can. Even though he's quickly becoming more attentive, other challenges

Did you know?

Feel like everyone's staring as your toddler shows his moody side? The average toddler has three meltdowns per hour, so chances are, onlookers have been there, done that. So the next time you're stuck in the supermarket line and your toddler throws a fit, just say to yourself, "I don't know these people. I'll never see them again." Then focus your energy on comforting your child.

– a new babysitter, a change in routine – can sometimes set him back a few developmental steps before he surges forward again.

How to have fun with it

No, tantrums are not fun – especially when they happen in public with lookers-on eyeing you disapproving. But they are par for the course in toddlerhood, so take a deep breath and remind yourself that your child won't be sprawled on the floor forever or gather him in your arms and tell him a story. Keep a special toy handy that you can use as a distraction when your little one has that occasional breakdown. Something as simple as a key ring with a little glowing light may prove to be an effective tantrum tamer.

> " A game of walking 'I Spy' ('I spy a red bicycle, do you see it?') got my 'terrible' toddler through most errands – and gave him a huge sense of accomplishment for being such a good 'spotter'. "
>
> – Debra, mother of three

Meltdowns may arise when your child has to go from one activity to another. Fun and games can smooth these transitions considerably. Make it a "race" to see which one of you can tidy up faster or put your jacket on first. If you have to leave the house against his wishes, let him choose a toy that he can bring with him or have a stash of on-the-go goodies that he only plays with in the car or buggy. Play can also be useful mid-tantrum. Again, thanks to a 2-year-old's short attention span, a puzzle, book, or

Stick to simple puzzles to avoid frustration.

favourite stuffed animal can be just what you need to distract the child with the flailing limbs and tears rolling down his face.

Children this age long to be masters of their universe. Allowing them to experience a measure of control and, within reason, increased independence can help head off tantrums. Give your toddler plenty of opportunities to do things by himself – like putting on his pyjamas, pouring his own juice, or carrying his own plate to the table. It's almost a guarantee that messes will follow, but try not to get upset; instead, enlist his help in the clean-up, which he may actually enjoy.

Suggest he choose what to play ("Do you want to dress up like a fireman or finger paint?") or ask, "Which dolls should we invite to the picnic?" Consult him about which park he wants to go to, and let him choose some of the snacks you'll bring. Let him boss you around a bit, too, by letting him create the games or make-believe world you're going to enter. Toddlers get a huge kick out of telling Mum and Dad what to do.

You can also help tame the frustration that your child experiences when he can't communicate effectively how he's feeling. At this age toddlers are just starting to understand that there actually are words to represent all those emotions bubbling up inside of them. In calm, tantrum-free moments, role-play that he's the parent and you're the child demanding a new ball at the toy store. When he says, "No!" use your best acting skills to show him how angry you are and say, "I'm really cross that you won't let me have that ball." His dolls or plush toys make excellent understudies in pretend situations, as do books about emotions and self-expression. Familiar stories or favourite movies often provide great "teachable moments" to point out how the characters are feeling: "Cinderella seems really sad that she can't go to the ball."

loving play

The new baby

What you'll notice

For every toddler who welcomes a new sibling with open arms, there are many more who take one look at the family's bundle of joy and tell it to "Go 'way!" Even the toddler who excitedly hugged Mummy's growing belly and talked to her little brother may feel and act very differently when her exhausted parents are preoccupied with the new arrival. She may regress in areas where she was making progress – crawling instead of walking, talking like a baby or crying instead of using her words, or clinging more than usual. Tantrums may occur more often and – unsurprisingly – may coincide with your need to feed or rock your newborn.

Aggression toward the baby is a normal reaction, which is why you have to maintain a watchful eye. Even when your toddler acts sweetly and lovingly towards her new sibling, be careful that her passionate hugs and kisses don't become a bit too rough.

On the flip side, your toddler may seem totally indifferent to the baby. Her detachment may signal a need to pretend this little interloper isn't there, or it could simply reflect that a newborn isn't the best playmate; after all, he doesn't do much besides sleep, cry, eat, and get his nappy changed.

Why it's happening

Well before you bring your baby home from the hospital, your toddler will sense that things are changing – and her uncertainty about what exactly is going on can be hard to handle. Once her sibling arrives, her behaviour – be it aggression or disinterest – reflects the fact that she now has to share your love and attention. And because a toddler's thinking is very concrete at this stage, she may wonder if there's enough to go around.

Acting out may simply be her way of figuring out her place in the family. When she sees the baby's bouncy seat or play mat in the area that used to be her exclusive domain, she may be resentful about having to share her space.

How to have fun with it

Fun is probably not the right word to describe dealing with your toddler's jealousy toward her sibling – especially when you're sleep-deprived. Make it easier by starting several weeks before the baby arrives. Use a doll or stuffed animal to act out what the baby will do and need. While you feed it, explain how babies need milk; when you tuck it in, explain that babies sleep a lot. Put a nappy on your newborn stand-in and get your child to help. Also, let her choose a stuffed animal or book for her new brother or sister so she feels like she's part of the welcome-home process. Research shows that parents who talk openly to their children before the new baby arrives and depict him or her as a real person, tend to have kids who adjust and get along better in the future.

When you come home from the hospital with your newborn, give your toddler her own bundle of joy to look after. There are many amazingly life-like baby dolls with physical features similar to a newborn: heavy heads and eyes that open and close. Having "someone" to

By pretending with her own baby, your child will identify better with you as you care for a new sibling.

Playing it safe

Increased aggression from a toddler towards a new baby in the family – handling her roughly or doing dangerous things like putting a pillow in her cot – is never permissible. Give your toddler opportunities to hold the baby while sitting in a supportive chair, but stay close by.

nurture while you're with your baby not only occupies your toddler while you're busy, but helps her better identify with you and her dad.

If your toddler is being aggressive or if she shouts, "No more baby!" commiserate rather than scold. When you say, "It's really hard sharing Mummy with the baby", your toddler feels understood, discovers it's okay to have these emotions, and learns that talking helps.

Along with cuddling time, your toddler needs plenty of one-on-one play with you. She also craves routines more than ever. If she's used to going to the playground every Saturday morning, ask a friend to spend an hour with the baby so you can take her.

Life with an emotional toddler and a needy newborn isn't easy. But learning to handle jealousy, anger, and other intense emotions she may be feeling is actually good for your toddler. She needs opportunities to exercise her cognitive and emotional muscles and adjusting to a shift in the family forces her to do just that. She will eventually adapt and come to love her lifelong playmate and ally.

healthy play

"I do it!" kid

What you'll notice

Your 2-year-old's constant refrain of "I do it" extends beyond walking without holding your hand, pouring his own cereal, or getting to an out-of-reach doll by pushing a chair over and climbing up. Now your little one will want to soap his body in the bath, brush his hair and teeth, and wash his hands. By the end of this year, he may insist on getting dressed without your help. His shirt may be backwards, his jersey inside out and his trousers unzipped and dangling somewhere near his knees, but he won't care. His smiling face will testify to the fact that what matters most is that he did it his way by himself.

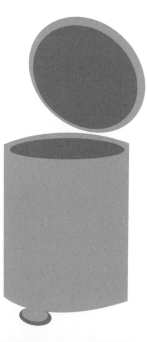

Why it's happening

Since those early weeks as a newborn, your child's been improving and refining his small-muscle control; now, between the ages of 2 and 3, he's really mastering the nuances of these fine-motor skills. Thanks to better manual dexterity and hand-eye coordination, your toddler can pick up (and put down) a brush or comb, hold a tube of toothpaste while lifting the flip-top, grip a toothbrush as he tries to manoeuvre it around his mouth, and pull a shirt over his head. He can also take off his shoes and socks (but it will be about a year before he can put them back on). And though he may not do these tasks perfectly or with ease, the combination of his newfound capabilities and quest for autonomy and control drive him to keep trying. Each time he succeeds and hears you praise his efforts, his confidence skyrockets, motivating him to up the ante.

These new skills and this budding independence aren't just good for keeping your toddler well-groomed. They help him hold a crayon better: mid-year you'll see his artwork go from abstract scribbles to recognizable images; he will build bigger brick towers and learn to hold a pair of children's scissors.

How to have fun with it

As long as he's offering, let your 2-year-old manage as much as possible. Songs and games can make self-care routines easier and more fun. For example, enlisting a puppet to hold your child's toothbrush – while talking in a funny voice – will inspire him to open wide. Find a song

Brushing teeth is one of the self-care skills a 2-year-old can practise daily.

to sing while your toddler is washing his hands. Do so for about 20 seconds – the recommended time for de-germing your hands. Two rounds of "Happy Birthday" will do the trick and changing the words to something like "Happy hand-washing to you" is bound to bring a smile.

On days when you simply don't have time for him to take ten minutes to brush his hair or put on a shirt, make a deal that you get to dress him, while he dresses his stuffed animal. Enhance his abilities in these areas by providing toys, books, and dolls designed to let him practise zipping, buttoning, tying, and opening. Or use play to speed things up: race to see who can find his shoes first.

Other things that help improve his fine motor skills include crayons or chalk and blunt scissors. Pull toys are a big hit at this age, because toddlers can look back as they walk – not to mention that their budding imaginations make that doggie or duck their very own pet.

Involving your 2-year-old in chores also builds his skills: armed with a child-size broom and dustpan, he will be an eager helper. And folding napkins or sorting cutlery exercises his fingers and his thinking muscles.

healthy play

I'm really jumping now

What you'll notice

It's hard to believe that just last year your child took her first wobbly steps. She can now walk on tip-toe, stop and start at will, change directions, vary her speed, and navigate around obstacles. At times, she may trip or stumble, but for the most part she's more agile than ever. Though she still walks down the stairs using two feet per step (rather than alternating them, as she will next year), she's getting proficient at climbing. She can scale the sofa and get back down all by herself and has a new passion for jungle gyms, slides, and stairs.

Your child can also squat to play with toys on the floor and easily get up from this position. Mid-year, she'll add another physical feat to her repertoire: jumping with her feet together.

At 2, children have the motor skills to learn to pedal a tricycle.

She can also pedal a tricycle – a freeing feeling that she loves. (It's the toddler's version of getting a driving license.)

Why it's happening

Her improved balance and coordination and advances in her gross-motor control mean she can do all this moving with ease. And because it's become so much easier (and is so exciting), she loves to be on the move. She's excited by her agility and wants to practise, practise, practise. However, her impulsive behaviour outstrips her ability to assess danger. For example, a toddler this age may dash over to the swings and get clocked in the head or try to scale a bookshelf and fall. By the time she's 3, she'll have a better sense of her surroundings and her own limits. In the meantime, it's critical to be nearby and alert while you allow her to explore. The difficult part for you is remembering that your child is not being defiant when she runs out into the middle of the street. It's simply the way she's wired at this age. Think of her brain as a driver with her foot all the way down on the accelerator and very weak brakes. Research shows that the prefrontal cortex, the part of the brain that's responsible for making good decisions, is still a work in progress.

How to have fun with it

Running games where your child starts, stops, and starts again are healthy activities that get her heart rate up and help to refine her skills. Having to wait for the "green light" also teaches impulse control. Chasing games are always a

Did you know?

Many parents find their 2-year-old to be more distractible, jumping from one toy or activity to the next. But it's not your toddler's attention span that's changing; it's her eyesight. Her peripheral vision improves and because she can see more things on the margins of her field of vision, there are more distractions.

hit or set up an obstacle course in the living room or outside. You can also put on music and have your children run around (or dance) like crazy until the music stops when they have to "Freeze!"

Try not to stifle her drive to explore and fine tune her skills. This means that you need to balance the admonitions to "be careful" with ample opportunities for her to run, climb, and jump at places like the park, indoor playgrounds, or gymnastics class. At home, set up play areas where your toddler has permission to jump and roll around.

Keeping up with an active toddler can make you feel like you're running a marathon, but it is critical for your child to release energy and build muscle. (Just think of all the calories you're burning!) And at a time when the rates of childhood obesity are through the roof (one in ten children are estimated to be overweight or obese in this country), it's critical to introduce exercise routines. Try going for family strolls or bike rides in the evenings or on weekends.

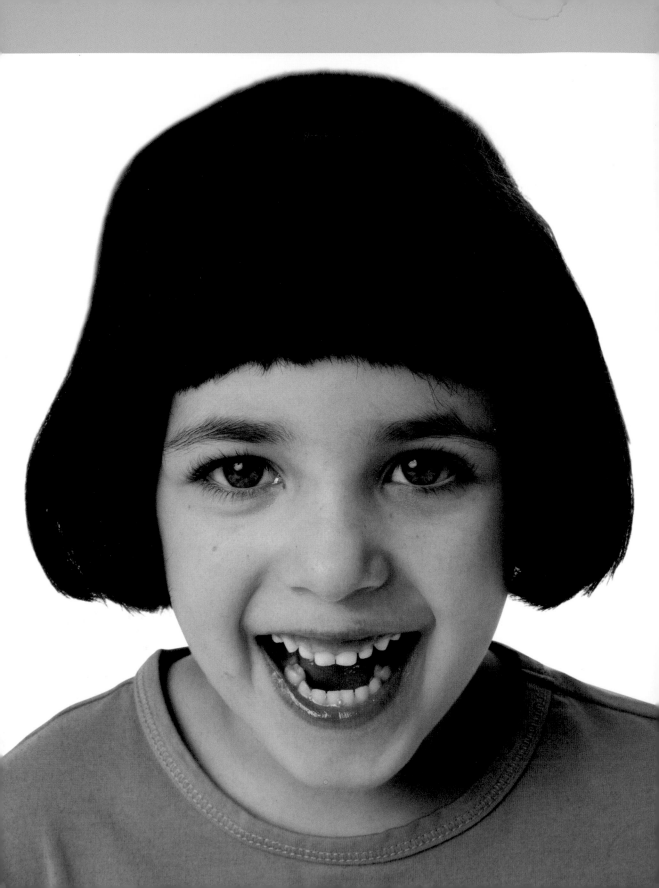

three-year-olds
The Magic Year

* * *

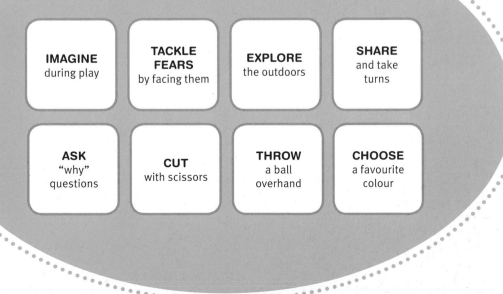

play milestones for this year

IMAGINE during play	**TACKLE FEARS** by facing them	**EXPLORE** the outdoors	**SHARE** and take turns
ASK "why" questions	**CUT** with scissors	**THROW** a ball overhand	**CHOOSE** a favourite colour

The Magic Year

If the first three years of a child's life are often
called "the wonder years", then this fourth
year should be dubbed "the magic year". Yes,
there's something charming about every age,
but 3-year-olds greet each day with a breathless,
wide-eyed attitude that seems to say, "Today is
going to be a fantastic adventure!" Whether
they're opening their toy box or the refrigerator,
rushing over to show you a drawing, or lathering
their hair with shampoo, they do so with a flourish
– as if every gesture deserves a drum roll, every
accomplishment a round of applause.

Watching your child this year, you'll be awed (and perhaps envious) of her limitless energy and enthusiasm. A ladybird holds her spellbound; a scarf transforms her into a glamorous sorceress; and the concoction she whips up out of mud, sticks, and a few blades of grass is almost good enough to eat. To a 3-year-old there aren't enough hours in the day (one reason why she may suddenly resist bedtime) and her spongelike mind makes her eager to absorb as much as she can from dawn until dusk.

Your child assumes that you share her sense of wonderment – and she never tires of exploring and explaining and asking about the world around her. She doesn't realize that you had a long day at the office or forgot to pick up the dry cleaning; all she knows is that she's an adventurer and you're her partner, teacher, coach, and playmate. Luckily for you, 3-year-old energy is infectious, and you'll probably find that joining her play is a great stress-buster.

Your pre-schooler now has the developmental skill and self-control to enjoy playing with other children and to sustain relationships with a growing circle of friends. Her physical abilities, such as increased coordination, balance, and strength coupled with advanced fine motor skills, add to the array of games and activities she and her peers enjoy.

Your child's budding imagination catalyzes an explosion in her creative play: her artwork is suddenly more detailed; her brick towers, more intricate; her pretend worlds, more complex. She'll go from reality to make-believe lands so seamlessly and with such gusto that you'll swear she really inhabits that castle, fairyland, or deep dark forest. Her insatiable curiosity will inspire a litany of questions that run the gamut from the creative ("Why is the moon a croissant tonight?") to the concrete ("Why do we have hair?"), but at times her wild imagination and intense curiosity may invite new fears and phobias – especially when it's "lights out".

The quizzical child

What you'll notice

Slip on your thinking cap, because this year your pre-schooler will be hosting a 24/7 version of Quiz Show – and you will be a regular guest. The rules of the game are simple: any time, any where, your child may pepper you with questions that will run the gamut from the sublime ("How do clouds get into the sky?") to the silly ("Why is ya ya ga ga?") to the embarrassing ("Why does that man have hair in his ears?"). You will often be expected to answer the same follow-up question ("Why?") at least a dozen times a day.

Why it's happening

Your child's curiosity is spurred by her imagination, which reaches new heights this year. The world around her is exciting and bewildering and she needs lots of information to make sense of it. At 2, she was happy playing in the bath and never questioned how the water got into the tub. Now she wants to know where it comes from, where it goes when she's done, and whether she might go down the drain with it. Before, she was content to jump in puddles; now she wonders how her reflection got in the puddle and why some puddles are muddy while others are clear. Armed with the language skills to ask what's on her mind, she wants to know how things work, what they're made of, where they're going next – and if she can't think of a way to formulate a new question, there's always that comfortable fall-back: "Why?"

Three-year-olds also have a longer attention span, so they can listen to your answers or absorb a story better, and their maturing memories enable them to relate new information to past experiences. Extremely social, 3-year-olds also discover that all this probing and "research" gets your attention.

A magnifying glass is a perfect tool for your little explorer.

How to have fun with it

No, you don't have to memorize the encyclopaedia or dust off your old school textbooks to answer your little scientist's questions. You do need to listen as patiently as you can (not always easy) and think about your responses. If you don't happen to know how the clouds got into the sky, compliment your pre-schooler for asking such a good question and suggest you find the answer together by looking in the encyclopaedia, researching it online, or going to the library. If you can't be bothered at that moment, say, "I'm not sure and we'll look it up when we're home, but if I had to guess I'd say …" Better yet, ask your child to guess why she thinks the clouds are there or where she thinks the water goes after she flushes the toilet. This will allow her to exercise her colourful imagination – and guarantees your appreciative laughter. Just make certain she doesn't think that you're laughing at her. And if you can, record your child's questions in a journal or memory book. You will enjoy looking back on this time as an age of inquisitiveness.

Games like "I Spy" or "20 Questions" are perfect for your Curious George (or Georgina), or you can play an easier version by providing a few traits about a person you both know and asking your child to guess who it is. Scavenger hunts in the woods or garden are also perfect activities for your intrepid explorer, especially if you arm her with child-sized binoculars, a butterfly net, or a magnifying glass.

learning play

Imagine that!

What you'll notice

Have a pen and notebook handy because you'll want to record as many of the amazing things your child makes up this year as possible. When he was 2, props often stimulated his pretend play: he would "cook" food in his pint-size kitchen or power his trucks over a mountain in the park. This year, he takes the next step and doesn't just use these objects for their intended use; he transforms them. Now, his kitchen is a place where a witch brews up poison and the buggy may be the display stand for fruit in his imaginary corner shop. And at times, he may not even need toys to play with since the worlds he can whip up in his mind are rich enough.

Because of this ability to "write" more elaborate stories and his longer focus and attention span, the way your child plays by himself shifts dramatically. He can sit for long periods of time, deeply engrossed in a fantasy world with his cast of plastic or wooden figures, jabbering away as he brings them to life under a chair in his room. Or he becomes the leading man in stories of his own creation. When your 3-year-old does this, he is not just pretending to be that superhero, he *is* that superhero. One look at his face and you'll see that he could just as easily be scaling tall buildings as he could be in your garden. Try not to interrupt: these worlds are quite private and if he senses you peering over his shoulder, he may stop playing.

On the other hand, he may introduce you to a new friend – one only he can see and hear. An estimated 65 per cent of children in this age group have imaginary pals, often with names and detailed profiles. In addition to providing comfort, imaginary playmates are convenient scapegoats for spilled milk or crayon marks on the wall: "Buzzy did it – not me!"

Why it's happening

Imaginary play is more than fun and games. It's a sign of your child's more advanced and adult-like thinking skills. Last year, he simply imitated actions that he had observed, such as feeding a baby or stacking bricks. This year, he moves on to what's called symbolic thinking where he can use one thing to represent another. For example, he pretends

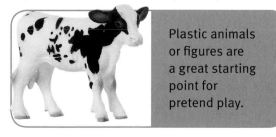

Plastic animals or figures are a great starting point for pretend play.

Homemade fun

Play a game called "Finish this story". Begin by setting the scene for a story, then give your child one minute to add to it. Then it's your turn to continue developing the plotline. Keep alternating like this and watch your child's imagination go wild.

a wooden brick is the toast he's making in his pretend kitchen or a tissue box is a cash register in his fantasy shop. Also, as a 3-year-old, he better remembers things he saw or experienced in the past and uses this real-world information as inspiration in his pretend one. His improved concentration means he can take part in a longer sequence of events (rather than repeating the same action over and over as he did last year) and his advanced language skills give him the words to create more detailed worlds both in his head and out loud.

Imaginary play may also be a big part of your child's life because most kids this age can't separate fantasy from reality. Though it's unclear exactly why this is so, one theory is that the two halves of a 3-year-old's brain – the right, which is responsible for perceptual skills, and the left, which is responsible for analytical skills – aren't working in sync yet (and probably won't be until around the age of 4).

Whether he is the actor in his own stories, creates imaginary scenes for his figures and stuffed animals, or has an imaginary friend, pretend play is helping him make sense of his world. After all, each day he is taking in a lot

> " When we're stuck in the car or out doing errands, I'll pick out a stranger and ask my child to tell me a story about his life. This works my son's imagination and provides hours of entertainment.
>
> – David, father of two "

of new information, something that can be quite overwhelming. Imaginary play helps him process and understand it better. For example, when he acts like Daddy leaving the house and going to the office, he communicates his feelings about saying goodbye; when he plays the teacher he sees what it's like to direct others.

How to have fun with it

Because your child's brain is like the proverbial sponge, his surroundings are a constant source of fascination and he can entertain himself pretty much anywhere, any time, and with anything. If all he has are three sticks, he'll make one the mummy, one the daddy, and one the baby, or a packet of sugar a pillow for his plastic man. Given his natural curiosity, it's almost a disservice to turn on the television or computer and take away from his sense of adventure and imagination. He needs and wants to use all his senses, and the more he is an active participant – rather than a passive recipient – in his play, the more he will learn.

Your 3-year-old is starting to notice differences in the world around him, which is why he knows that a doctor wears one kind of uniform while a firefighter wears another or why he pretends to have long hair when he's Mummy, but short hair when he's Daddy. To build upon this understanding, read books about different types of people from various countries experiencing a range of activities and provide dolls from different cultures. Encourage him to notice the variations in nature by looking at different types of insects, rocks, leaves, and trees. Child-size butterfly nets and garden explorer kits can make this even more fun.

Before you pack up the toys and props from your child's toddler years, keep in mind that the dramatic advances in his development mean he will now interact with old toys in new and different ways. Last year, that paper towel roll was simply something he used like a telescope; this year he will transform it into a sword, a tree, a pet snake – all in one day. The miniature broom he uses to help you with chores will double as a guitar, a laser or a flag in his fort. Dressing-up clothes; play tents (often in shapes like castles and pirate ships); restaurant kits; plush bags that come filled with pretend keys, lipstick, and mobile phones; chunky tools; faux cash registers; pretend food; doll sets complete with nappies, bibs, and bottles; picnic and tea sets; and miniature vacuum cleaners are all great props for pretend play. This year, he'll go from cuddling stuffed toys to giving them roles in his stories, so he'll love plastic or wood or plush versions of his favourite characters and animals.

When it comes to an imaginary pal, don't try to convince your child that this invisible buddy isn't real (so does not need his own seat at the table). It's best to just play along, including telling "Buzzy" that if he spilled the milk, he needs to clean it up. You can also use this friend to help your child manage challenging experiences. If a visit to a new daycare centre or a doctor's office seems to be causing stress, have your child explain to his imaginary friend what to expect. Or if you're trying to wrestle him into his pyjamas, turn your attention to "Buzzy" and announce the start of the Great PJ Race. Just make sure your pre-schooler wins!

Playing it safe

Take Mum's high heels out of the dressing-up box and hem any clothes that may be too long – both are tripping hazards. Also, replace any pins, brooches, or badges with sharp clasps with more child-friendly accessories.

loving play

Sharing and caring

What you'll notice

Last year, your toddler made the big leap from parallel to more reciprocal play. At 2, she probably observed other children from the sidelines before jumping into the action and still needed your help getting comfortable with her peers. But now that she's a pre-schooler, she's more at ease and excited about being with other children. Though she probably won't really master sharing until her fourth birthday, she's definitely loosening her grip on her stuff.

The way your child and her friends interact will also change. Now they'll talk, laugh and enter one another's pretend worlds. You may even find that your child promotes one or two children to the rank of "best friend" (even if she doesn't know exactly what that means). Though you have probably decided who will fill her social calendar in the past, now she'll request dates with certain children.

One heartwarming aspect of your child's behaviour in the friendship arena is how easily and enthusiastically she makes friends. Within minutes of arriving at the playground, your 3-year-old will be collaborating on a track for her new friend's plastic horse or marching happily arm and arm over to the slide. In contrast to unfamiliar adults at a dinner party, threes rarely engage in stilted small talk; they get right down to the business of having fun. (Interestingly, your child may do this even if she tends to be slow to warm up with adults.)

Why it's happening

Your pre-schooler is a better playmate because she's developing skills like taking turns and sharing. Her ability to delay gratification will develop further over the next few years – but she is starting to under-stand the give and take that relationships require. By her half birthday, it will probably be easier to wait her turn for the swing or for her chance to wear her friend's fairy crown.

Toys, like play food, promote sharing when they come in pairs.

Your child's problem-solving skills make it easier for her to resolve conflicts and to coordinate her play with her friends. For example, a young pre-schooler may still grab a toy, but when her friend then refuses to play with her, she learns to use a different approach.

Some 3-year-olds have an easier time than others when it comes to reading social cues. Depending on your child's temperament, she may be more sensitive to rejection or have a low tolerance for frustration that will impact her ability to sustain extended playtimes. But most children this age discover the delight in joining their buddies in elaborate fantasy worlds. One friend may say, "Let's be aeroplanes" and another will immediately spread his wings. This pretend play is less choreographed than it will be next year when they may discuss where to go and what to do there, but it's clearly more enjoyable than taking a solo flight.

Studies suggest that your pre-schooler will learn around a dozen new words daily. And her expanded vocabulary results in better self-expression and comprehension. Combined with her enhanced imagination, her communication abilities will enable your child and her pals to talk more, make up stories, and tell each other jokes (with punch lines only a 3-year-old could love).

loving play

The age of enthusiasm

What you'll notice

Passionate, effusive, energetic, enthusiastic – children this age approach life with zest, zeal, and excitement. When you come home, your pre-schooler throws his arms around you and plants juicy kisses on your cheek. The hugs he gives his friends are so zealous he sometimes knocks them over. And his daily discoveries are met with the pre-school equivalent of "Eureka!"

His toys and dolls are also objects of his affection. Whether it's a cuddly stuffed animal or a pointy metal truck, you may see him pick it up and lovingly cradle it. This is also a time when your child may develop an obsession with something, such as a favourite tee shirt he has to wear every day or a cartoon character he knows all about. Or maybe he's fallen for a colour that dictates his choice in everything from the clothes he wears to the foods he eats.

> "My daughter's language is exploding and the way she expresses herself is so adorable that I've started recording her on video. I turn the camera on when she's not aware so I can capture her at her most spontaneous.
> – Pam, mother of two"

He doesn't just show this affection with his body language; he uses his words. When you tuck him in at night, his unsolicited whisper of "I love you" will leave a lump in your throat. He also proclaims his passion for everything from his babysitter to his blanket.

The positive spin your pre-schooler puts on everything breathes new life into old favourites. Coming across a toy he's seen a million times, he will pick it up and exclaim, "My dinosaur puzzle!" as if it's brand new.

Why it's happening

Your 3-year-old's ability to notice details expands dramatically this year. He puts his heart into everything he does and approaches the world with such enthusiasm because he does see something new each time he looks around. His physical skills, like strength and coordination are also improving, so he's able to do more in his environment, to pick up and manipulate things he finds and to share those discoveries with his growing circle of pals.

More independent than he's been in his whole (albeit, short) life, he may now grasp how big the world he lives in can seem – an overwhelming concept, which can usher in a need for predictability and control. A favourite item of clothing he demands to wear every day or a familiar toy or cartoon character can serve as a comforting anchor during this period of dramatic growth.

How to have fun with it

You may be tired of the colour yellow, a favourite cartoon character, or your child choosing the same toy or book over and over (and over) again. But let your child have his obsession. This intense focus is another way that he soaks up information and learns. By living in a purple-only world he's learning about different textures, shapes, and properties of all things that come in that colour. By playing with that same puzzle or reading that same book, he's also gaining new knowledge each time.

Preference for a favourite colour often comes through at age 3.

healthy play

Working with my hands

What you'll notice

Your 3-year-old's creative juices are flowing and her almost adult-like grip on her crayon transforms the scribbles of last year into drawings that feature an array of stick figures and recognizable shapes. As the months pass, her drawing skills will evolve and she'll be able to create a bigger cast of characters and add interesting details like hair and clothes. She's a master with a colouring book, staying within the lines when she wants to. And once she conquers scissors, their fascination will inspire her to snip with abandon – sometimes just to see what happens. Arm her with a glue stick or a jar of paste and deck the walls with an outpouring of collages and artistic creations.

In general, your child is better at balancing and stacking bricks and assembling and arranging things. She can snap one plastic brick into another, thread large beads or macaroni onto string, or mould pieces of play dough together.

Why it's happening

Certainly, her blossoming imagination is part of what's unleashed your child's inner artist. But her improved fine-motor control, hand-eye coordination, and spatial skills are what allow her to hold a small crayon, cut a simple shape out of paper, pick up tiny things like sequins and glue them onto paper. She may be ahead of her male peers in these areas, because girls typically develop these fine motor skills earlier than boys. But if your son is struggling to get that brick tower just so, be patient. It will happen.

She doesn't know what she's drawing before she puts crayon to paper, but will be glad to describe it to you in detail when she's done. While using her hands to create, your child is continuing the study of textures, shapes, and colours that started back in her cot. And just as those early tactile experiences had an impact on her developing brain, your pre-schooler's exposure to lots of different materials boosts her cognitive skills dramatically.

How to have fun with it

A well-stocked art box is ideal for your 3-year-old. Fill it with play dough, crayons, paper, scissors, colouring books, stencils, glue sticks, stamps and ink pads, and stickers. Now that your child is a little older, you may want to add new mediums, like magic markers and paints. Though these seem like accidents waiting to happen, "big kid" tools boost her confidence and enhance her creativity. To keep messes to a minimum, practise a policy of containment: devote a special place in the house to creative

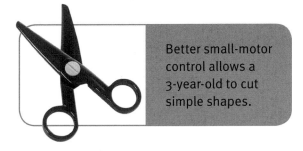

Better small-motor control allows a 3-year-old to cut simple shapes.

projects – a child-size table and chairs, and nearby shelves stocked with materials, or a corner of the kitchen next to a drawer of supplies. Buy a couple of cheap shower curtains or plastic tablecloths to spread on the floor.

Less is often more when it comes to sparking creativity, especially in pre-schoolers, who may find a small amount of glue on a divided paper plate much less intimidating than a whole bottle, which requires holding, squeezing, and aiming to get just right.

No matter what you're creating with your child, resist the urge to correct her. If she puts the googly eye on the snowman's stomach or uses more glue than glitter in her collage, so be it. Experimenting without rules and restrictions is helping her to learn.

Enhance your pre-schooler's fine-motor skills and coordination by giving her lots of practice with things like zips, big buttons, and snaps – both by letting her dress herself and by providing toys, books, and dolls designed to teach these skills. Let her help you with household tasks that work her fingers – wrapping up leftovers or pouring juice from a small plastic jug into her cup. Ask her to fold paper napkins to put on the dinner table or help you tear lettuce for a salad.

healthy play

Getting it together

What you'll notice

Where did the time go? That's what you'll ask yourself as you watch your pre-schooler run and jump with ease. Now he can pick up speed as he rides his tricycle, throw a ball overhand, and catch a large ball – usually by putting out both arms and trapping it against his chest. Gone are the days when he needed to hold your hand to climb the stairs; today, he can do so while alternating feet and even jump from the bottom step. In fact, climbing is his forte, and you'll be amazed at his agility on

> "On rainy days, I set up a little goal in our living room and let my son practise kicking a ball into it while I play goalie. It's not a big field, but it works!
> – Zoe, mother of one

all the playground equipment. He zooms to the top of the slide, swings higher and faster by pumping his legs rhythmically, and kicks a ball backward and forward.

Why it's happening

In your child's first year, his birth weight tripled and his height grew by 50 per cent. Back then, his head was also much larger than the rest of his body while his legs were relatively smaller and shorter. This year, your child still makes gains in height and weight, but at a slower rate, while his body becomes more proportionate. His head is no longer growing at a rapid pace (it reaches 90 per cent of its adult size by age 2) so it doesn't look oversized in comparison to the rest of him. At the same time, his arms and legs grow longer and stronger and he begins to shed that baby fat (something that may actually make you a little sad). These more

even proportions shift his centre of gravity closer to the middle of his body (rather than near his chest, like it was when he was a baby). Such big physical changes mean that your child has more strength, body control, coordination, agility, and balance.

How to have fun with it

Moving his body is no longer something he has to work so hard at – so he'll naturally enjoy running, jumping, and climbing games. Towards the end of this year, when he has even better body and impulse control, you can play games like "Red Light, Green Light", tag, musical chairs, and "Simon Says".

Bring him outdoors to kick a ball back and forth and play catch. He can also climb on his tricycle or foot-powered ride-on toys, which not only strengthen his legs, but provide a new prop for some fun imaginary play. Take family walks or let him ride his bike while you power walk or jog. Set up obstacle courses outside for him to run or ride his bike through. Of course, chasing each other around is even more fun now that your child has picked up speed, and you may be stunned to realize that you have to work pretty hard to catch him!

Your child is learning to throw overhand and to catch.

healthy play

Bedtime battles

What you'll notice

Your once early-to-bed child now puts up a fight at the mere mention of pyjamas. Sometimes she runs off and hides or starts crying because she wants to play. Your 5-minute warning gets whined into 10. And when you finally pick her up, she's a lot faster, stronger, and squirmier than your patience and energy can handle. The same unpleasant dance may occur at naptime – even if she's rubbing her eyes and looks like she's about to nod off.

Why it's happening

With a big, wide world to explore, the last thing your child wants to do is waste time sleeping. Bursting with curiosity, engrossed in a make-believe world, or suddenly fascinated by the lint under the sofa, she doesn't want to hear that it's time for bed. And though she has a better sense of time and space, tomorrow seems like an eternity.

Also, because she's at a stage where she may be experiencing fears and phobias, "lights-out" may be an unwelcome invitation for her to conjure up scary visitors. Sometime this year your child may stop needing a day-time nap, because she requires less sleep than she did during her baby and toddler years.

How to have fun with it

Borrow a technique from pre-school teachers and make a card with your child's name and picture on it. Then place this label on top of whatever she is playing with before bed or naptime. This way she can rest assured that no one will be having fun with her toys while she's catching her forty winks and that she can pick up right where she left off when she wakes up.

Refusing to nap may be a sign that she is ready to drop this midday siesta. Still, insist that she have some quiet time on her bed – not necessarily to sleep, but to read or play quietly. Often just being on her bed will make her drowsy or provide a much-needed break and relax her body. Even when the nap is gone for good, this quiet hour should remain a routine during which she learns to entertain herself and recharge her batteries.

Create rituals to help your child settle down for bed, like taking a bath before bed each night.

Did you know?

A drop in body temperature signals the brain that it's time to sleep. So if your child goes straight from a warm bath to a warm bed, she may have trouble drifting off to dreamland. A bath an hour or so before bed gives your child's body time to cool down and prepare her brain for sleep.

Television or a film should not be part of a child's bedtime ritual. A better choice is soft, gentle music. And keep rough-housing or active play to a minimum at least an hour before bedtime. Create routines. It's something that you'll hear at every stage but plays a particularly vital role during the pre-school years, when children need about 10 to 12 hours of sleep. If bath time is always followed by a book, prayers, or a special quiet game like saying goodnight to all of her stuffed animals, her brain and body are primed to calm down long before the lights go out.

four-years-olds
The Feeling Fine Phase

* * *

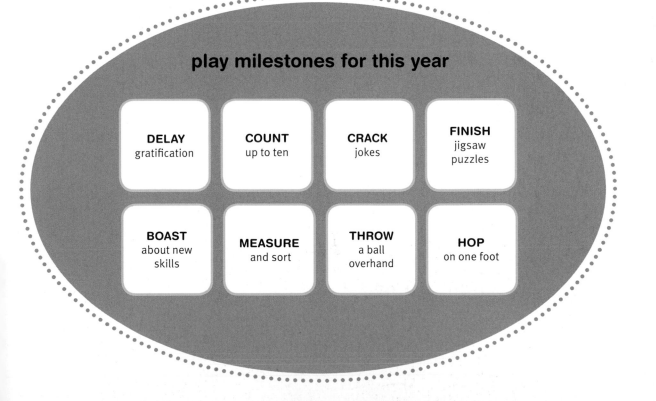

play milestones for this year

DELAY
gratification

COUNT
up to ten

CRACK
jokes

FINISH
jigsaw
puzzles

BOAST
about new
skills

MEASURE
and sort

THROW
a ball
overhand

HOP
on one foot

The Feeling Fine Phase

With each passing birthday, your little one has grown from a chubby-cheeked baby to an unsteady toddler to an increasingly independent child. The difference this year is that you're not the only one dazzled by this transformation: your 4-year-old understands that her baby days are behind her. "Know what I can do?" she will ask, before eagerly showing off her ability to count to ten or throw a ball overhand or ride a bike with training wheels.

Your child has many reasons to blow her own trumpet. Thanks to her longer attention span, improved hand-eye coordination, manual dexterity, and enhanced cognitive skills, she adds to her repertoire of playtime activities more advanced board and card games, puzzles, and art projects. The challenges these pose and the skills they require make playtime more enjoyable for both of you. It's exciting to introduce your child to games that you loved when you were young and to share her glee when she beats you down the path in the favourite board game from your youth. Eager to be "the best", she may still have a hard time losing and may bend the rules occasionally.

These more interesting games, along with play that involves building and balancing or activities like cooking that require pouring and measuring, expand upon skills like number recognition, sorting, grouping, and counting. These further develop traits that will benefit her for a lifetime: patience and self-discipline. Learning to control one's impulses and delay gratification are critical challenges of childhood, affecting everything from learning to forging friendships. And as your child heads toward her fifth birthday, she will get better at managing frustration and weathering difficult times.

One of the great delights of this year will be the emergence of your 4-year-old's sense of humour. Riddles and jokes that foil her expectations or challenge her to use her imagination will lose nothing in the retelling; she's guaranteed to find her own jokes and antics wildly amusing. And the joy of making other people laugh – including her peers – will usher in a new phase in her relationships with friends. Although most of the time you will laugh right along, some of what tickles her funny bone may rub you the wrong way – especially when she's giggling about subjects best reserved for the bathroom. You may also be troubled by your 4-year-old's first foray into bad behaviour, such as excluding a friend, acting aggressively during play, or talking back to you – an attitude you may have associated with the teenager years.

Not only does your child act older, she looks older. Her facial features and physique appear more grown up – no more chubby cheeks and protruding belly – and her muscles are stronger, enabling her to climb, run, jump, skip, and hop without stumbling. The confidence she experiences from these dramatic physical leaps inspires her to take on more challenges – even those for which she may not be quite ready – so keep an eye on your wonderful whirling dervish.

learning play

Waiting games

What you'll notice

Your child asks you for some apple juice and when you reply, "Just a minute", he will actually wait considerably longer than he did when he was 3. Playing a game, he's less impatient as he waits his turn. And when that brick tower comes tumbling down, he expresses mild frustration before starting over again. His progress in exercising patience and delaying gratification will reap major benefits as he heads off to school and is required to queue up, share with other children, or sit in a circle on the floor. Controlling his impulses, developing self-discipline, learning to persist with a task, and dealing with frustration are not easy skills to master, and some children (and many adults) have a harder time than others.

> **"** One of my favourite summertime routines with my son is to sit in a big outdoor chair at dusk and watch the stars come out. As impatient as he can be during the day, that darkening sky calms and soothes him.
>
> – Ann, mother of two **"**

One well-known study conducted at Stanford University in the 1960s looked at how important delayed gratification is to lifelong success. Individual 4-year-olds were told that they could have one marshmallow right away or get two of these sweet treats if they waited 15 to 20 minutes. The researcher then stepped out of the room, leaving the 4-year-old alone with the marshmallows. About one-third of the children couldn't resist grabbing one immediately, while another third held out until the researcher returned. (The other third were somewhere in between.) When researchers followed these children into adulthood, they found that those who exhibited impulse control as pre-schoolers were more self-disciplined, motivated, and positive as adults. They could also handle frustration and delay gratification better than their more impulsive peers and enjoyed more satisfying marriages, successful careers, better health, and higher incomes.

Why it's happening

By now, experience has taught your child that he is more likely to get what he wants if he is patient. He also has a better sense of time (so he knows what a minute feels like), and a longer attention span to help him wait it out. At 4, your child realizes that other people have feelings, too, and his empathic understanding helps him negotiate the give and take necessary to take turns during a game of cards with a friend. Though he really wants to pick a card, he knows it's his friend's turn and he needs to wait. Having said that, some children are more impatient and have less self-control, partly because the area of the brain that's responsible for controlling impulses and

Multi-step projects like assembling a Playmobil set build patience.

making "executive decisions" is still a work in progress at this age. This is especially true if the game is taking place right before lunch or when one of the pals is tired and irritable.

How to have fun with it

Don't worry if your 4-year-old would have gobbled up that marshmallow in an instant. Certain activities and games can help her build the cognitive muscles needed to delay gratification. Though board games that require turn-taking are helpful, so are activities that don't offer immediate payoffs. Baking and cooking take plenty of advance preparation and patience – waiting for those biscuits to bake and then to cool. Craft projects, multi-step games, jigsaw puzzles, and building sets that take time to assemble stretch the same muscles. Or try projects that take days or weeks to produce results such as Chia pets, ant farms, or planting a vegetable garden.

Opportunities to help your child learn to delay gratification arise countless times during the day – whenever she asks for something, in fact. Requiring her to wait a minute and then complimenting her on her patience, teaching her not to interrupt when others are talking, or standing back when she's struggling to put on her shoes, are little ways you can make a big difference in her ability to tolerate frustration.

To help your pre-schooler cope with longer waits – an upcoming trip to the aquarium, visit from a relative, birthday, or holiday – create a calendar that shows the current date and how long until the anticipated event. Each morning, your child can cross off a day and experience the excitement of looking forward to something. You can also make a countdown chain: use strips of construction paper to form a linked chain, each link representing one day. Let her tear off a link every morning and count the number of days that remain.

As with many other "virtues" we would like our children to develop, patience must be modelled. If your child seems to have a short fuse, pay attention to the ways that you and other adults in her world handle frustration. Do you honk the horn the second the traffic light changes to green? Lose your temper when your computer is especially slow? Most importantly,

Did you know?

Biologists and anthropologists say that impatience is an inherent impulse that has contributed to the survival of the species. By demanding attention, a child ensures that her needs for food and care are met and also forges a stronger attachment to Mum and Dad. She'll naturally overcome this impatience, provided that you help her learn how to cope with frustration.

how do you handle your child when she's dawdling or when she makes a mistake? Find ways to model coping strategies, and be as explicit as possible: when you're creeping along at 5 miles per hour, turn on the radio and explain that music calms you down. Or bring something to read (for both you and your child), so when you are running errands and get delayed, you have something to do while you're stuck in the queue.

At home, use a kitchen timer or a clock with a second hand to help your child visualize how long she has to wait. And if you say, "We will go to the park as soon as the bell rings", stay true to your promise.

If your child is not in any kind of activities programme, consider enrolling her in some form of pre-school. Even if she only attends a few times a week, she will be taught self-control and how to wait her turn – essential skills that will prepare her for "big" school.

learning play

A zillion and counting

What you'll notice

When your 4-year-old is eating pasta, she counts the pieces on her spoon; when she walks toward the car, she tallies up how many steps it takes to get there. She can recite numbers up to at least ten (to twenty by the end of the year) and may even be able to write those from zero to nine.

During board games, your budding mathematician is fascinated by what number the dice will land on, shouting out "Six!" and enthusiastically marching her game piece ahead.

She is also intrigued by patterns and sorting – separating her M&Ms by colour, grouping her plastic bricks into "grown-up" or "baby" piles, arranging her stuffed animals from smallest to tallest. Give her your loose change: she'll happily sort out the pennies.

By the second half of this year, she'll be able to identify simple patterns and enjoy picking up where you left off. When it comes to numbers, she likes talking about the biggies – think millions, trillions, infinity, and her own adorable improvisations, such as "one million hundred". She'll also understand the concepts of "tallest biggest, same, more", although she may have a hard time accepting that a tall man can be younger than a shorter one. Her brick-building techniques will change, too, as she employs more sophisticated problem solving and logic to stack and join structures so they stay balanced and grow more complex.

Why it's happening

Last year, your child may have impressed you with her counting skills, but she was probably just reciting numbers without understanding them. This year, she will grasp important numerical rules; for example, she understands that a symbol like "2" represents objects – two socks or two ice cream cones. She knows how to count in order, that the last number equals how many objects there are in a group, and that anything can be counted from concrete things like marbles to abstract ones like the beeps of a car's horn.

Four-year-olds also have improved spatial skills, which means that they can put jigsaw puzzles together and describe or draw simple maps or diagrams. Part of the reason why your child can grasp these mathematical concepts is that this year, the two halves of her brain – the right (responsible for perceiving patterns and understanding big concepts) and the left (sequential, analytical, and orderly) – begin working together more efficiently.

Children this age are highly sensitive to the attitudes and behaviour of those they love. A child whose mum regularly complains "I'm rubbish at maths!" may absorb a similarly self-defeating attitude. Homes where games and activities include lots of opportunites to talk about numbers and quantities naturally nurture children's love of mathematics.

How to have fun with it

Board games that don't require reading – like Candy Land and Snakes and Ladders – give your child practice in identifying numbers, counting, and sequencing, while card games teach your child how big numbers are in relation to one another. Some research

Play with games and puzzles that include numbers to sharpen counting skills.

suggests that how well your child does in primary school maths is linked to how many board and card games you have played together. Made-up games help, too. Teach her how the symbol of a number (e.g., 4) relates to objects by rolling dice and asking her to find something in that quantity around the house or outside, such as four spoons, pebbles, or dolls.

Household chores offer plenty of potential maths lessons. Set the table together, asking her to count out the number of place settings or to tell you how many slices there are in a pie. While food shopping, she can count how many yogurts you put in the trolley and how many people are in the queue in front of you. Let her compare foods by asking which of two items is heavier, smaller, or rounder. When you are folding laundry, ask her to sort the clothes in different ways, such as by colour, size, or style. Also, explain the sequence of events when you're doing something and get her to do the same. For example, "First, I sort the dark clothes from the white ones, second, I put them into the machine, and third, I add the powder."

Cooking and baking are other ways to indulge a 4-year-old's passion for counting, sorting, and measuring while also teaching her about things like fractions. Read recipes out loud and help her fill the measuring cup. If recipes are visual (like those on the back of some cake and brownie mixes), let her "read" how many eggs or sticks of butter are needed.

When you're on the phone or busy, give your child multi-coloured buttons or beans to sort, count, or arrange in a pattern. Or get a kit of beads – which she now has the manual dexterity and hand-eye coordination to thread onto string – and ask her to make a necklace or bracelet with a specific pattern. Coloured bricks and cubes or train tracks that snap or fit together naturally demonstrate what happens when you add or subtract. And, if you hand over a child-safe tape measure, she'll spend hours sizing up everything from a pencil to a piano.

An important maths-related skill, visual imagery, refers to the ability to create and hold onto mental pictures. Develop this in your child by playing a game where each of you has to describe a place you've visited recently. Use details and colour: for example, if she's describing the doctor's waiting room, ask what kind of toys were on the floor, what colour the chairs were, and if she remembers anything that was on the walls.

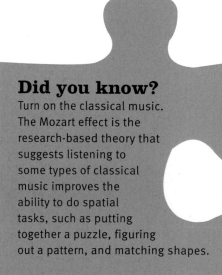

Did you know?
Turn on the classical music. The Mozart effect is the research-based theory that suggests listening to some types of classical music improves the ability to do spatial tasks, such as putting together a puzzle, figuring out a pattern, and matching shapes.

"My son's toys are organized into clear plastic bins. It's easy for him to see what goes where (bricks, animals, action figures) so he enjoys sorting while we clean up together.

— Meredith, mother of two

learning play

Finding her funny bone

What you'll notice

Expect to laugh a lot this year when your energetic child discovers her inner comedian. She loves playing the fool, making funny faces, singing silly songs, using made-up words, and exaggerating wildly. Knock-knock jokes (classics and her own creations) are a favourite of the 4-year-old set. The punch lines may make no sense to you and other adults, but her peers will appreciate them, and she'll laugh loudly at her own jokes, too. Potty talk is a major source of hilarity. Anything related to poo, pee, and her private parts can send her into stitches, and she'll have no qualms raising her voice to raise a few eyebrows in public. But by far her favourite audience is you: laugh at a silly joke and your little one will repeat it over and over again.

Why it's happening

Your child's vocabulary consists of hundreds of words and she can create sentences up to eight words long. Combined with her vivid imagination, her linguistic skills make telling jokes and inventing silly sentences a rich and rewarding way to connect with the people she loves. Because she knows the "right" answers to lots of questions, she finds blurting out the "wrong" ones instantly entertaining. Recognizing the pattern and rhythm in a knock-knock joke, she's perceptive enough to mimic it – even if the punch line makes no sense. And when the cartoon cat on her favourite TV programme is once again foiled by the mouse, she definitely appreciates the gag.

Despite her growing vocabulary, potty-related words top her list because toilet training may be on her mind – even if she's been out of nappies for a while. She may also pick up these phrases from her friends – especially those with older siblings. Most of all, your 4-year-old now has a sense of what's appropriate to say and what's not. Breaking those rules and seeing your startled response to a blurted "bad word" gives her a thrill. Even if you're shocked

Donning a pair of funny glasses or an amusing hat will send a 4-year-old reeling with laughter.

and annoyed, she's definitely got your attention – and she'll keep it up.

How to have fun with it

Your 4-year-old is definitely not the first child to scream "poo-head" in the library or at church. Don't stifle her desire to make others laugh; instead, tell her she can go into the bathroom to say those words. (Yelling "bad words" alone in the bathroom gets tedious really fast!) If she blurts out something inappropriate in public, try not to react. Chances are that when her story about burping fails to get a rise out of you, she'll move on to a more suitable subject.

Encourage good, clean fun with props that bring out her silly side: funny glasses and hats or books and music with puns and other word-play. Be an eager audience when she wants to show off the quirky songs or dances she's choreographed. Developing a repertoire of family jokes is one of the joys of parenthood and can be a godsend when your child is mid-meltdown or in a bad mood. (A joke or silly phrase can do the same for you.) And remember that cracking up is good for your child's health and your own. Research suggests that laughing reduces stress, lowers blood pressure, releases feel-good endorphins, boosts the immune system, and helps you breathe more deeply.

Did you know?

Don't send in the clowns. Researchers at the University of Sheffield set out to study what they could do to boost the mood at hospital children's wards. When researchers interviewed 250 patients ranging in age from 4 to 16 years old, they found that the children saw nothing funny about clowns. In fact, they unanimously disliked them and found them disturbing or scary.

loving play

Look at me! Look at me!

What you'll notice

Modesty is probably not a virtue you'd ascribe to your 4-year-old and, in that, you're not alone. Most children this age strut their stuff with an enviable air of confidence; their body language seems to say, "Look at me! Look at me!" and they love to boast about their many talents and accomplishments. It may surprise you the first time you hear your child brag that she can swing the highest or has the most toys. She'll challenge other kids by saying, "I can go down the big slide. Can you?" or "Let's race. I bet I'm the fastest." She may exaggerate her abilities, and invoke the face-saving phrase "Best of three?" when she doesn't quite pull off a task or when she loses at a game.

Why it's happening

By the age of 4, your pre-schooler is aware of her abilities and how they stack up against her peers. Last year, she watched the "big kids" zoom across the monkey bars; this year she can do it, too. Last year, the big kids pedalled past her tricycle; this year she's traded up for a bike with training wheels. These successes send her self-esteem soaring. She's proud and amazed and wants the world to know how competent she is. If she doesn't get that approval from others, she may boast as a way of praising herself.

How to have fun with it

When our children are young, it's easy to confuse high self-esteem with feeling good all the time. In fact, the experiences that build self-esteem often involve setbacks, disappointment, or frustration. The child whose parent stands back while she struggles to get the bricks stacked high experiences a much sweeter "reward" than a child who is rescued by a grown-up's steadier hand. Encourage similar experiences by letting your little one deal with frustration when she's learning something new or when she needs gentle prodding to persist with a tough task.

Praise may seem like the best way to make your child feel worthy and competent, but research shows that this depends on how you dole out the compliments and what you say. To make her feel good about her accomplishments, focus on the process – what she did or how she did it – rather than the final product.

Did you know?

A boastful 4-year-old is the norm, as children do not develop a sense of modesty until around 8 years of age. Interestingly, once they do begin to exhibit humility, they are more inclined to show reserve when talking to their peers than when they are talking to adults. They seem to catch onto the social stigma that labels self-promoters untrustworthy.

Saying, "Great job", when she hasn't tried very hard, or broadly complimenting her ("You're so clever!"), are far less effective motivators than honest and specific comments. Point out what you like about her picture: "I love that you put polka dots on the elephant", or "My favourite part is the sky". Or praise her effort with a simple, "Wow! You worked so hard on that puzzle!" rather than telling her she's the "best 4-year-old at puzzles" you've ever seen.

Another confidence booster is your full and undivided attention. Nothing makes your pre-schooler feel more important than when you stop multi-tasking to really listen when she talks or watch her when she shows off a new feat. Anything that makes your 4-year-old feel like a big kid is also a self-esteem booster, so encourage her to order her own dessert at a restaurant, hand money to the assistant at a shop, or answer the phone.

Puzzles take perseverance. When she struggles, resist the urge to help her.

loving play

Not all sugar 'n' spice

What you'll notice

Chances are that your child's play was relatively calm when he was 3. There may have been occasional heroics, but not too much aggression or violence. This year, he and his friends may wrestle and tumble, play war games, and pepper their play with expressions like, "I'm going to kill you!" (Though it sounds stereotypical, boys tend to engage in this type of behaviour more than girls.) All of this can be quite alarming and make you long for the teddy-bear tea parties of the past. Your pre-schooler may act bossy, mean (excluding a child or announcing, "I don't like you"), or aggressive. Telling tales on others is more common this year, too. Worse, your often sweet and loving child may be rude or disrespectful and towards the end of this year you may hear the dreaded "I hate you".

Why it's happening

For years now you've been telling your child to use his words and now he's doing just that. On the bright side, instead of reacting to feelings of anger or frustration by having a meltdown, biting, or hitting, he's exercising his verbal skills to express his emotions. And like potty talk, acting mean or rude often elicits a shocked reaction from others; for any child seeking attention, a negative response is better than no response at all.

Aggression or anger during play may also be your child's attempt to sort through feelings about something that's bothering him. For example, a child who is struggling to adjust to a new sibling may take out his jealous anger on a doll; a 4-year-old who's nervous about pre-school may pretend to be a bossy teacher.

Don't worry that your aggressive or bossy 4-year-old is destined to be the playground bully. Excluding another child is common, especially when your child and his friend have been playing one-on-one and have developed a rhythm and

Aggressive play with toys like scary dinosaurs help kids work through their feelings.

together – a race to the swings, a game of catch – but if that doesn't work, help the other child find something to do. Then later, in a private moment with your 4-year-old, talk about what happened, then provide a nicer "script" he can use the next time.

Pre-screen TV programmes and older siblings' video games to make sure that they don't contain highly aggressive (or other inappropriate) behaviour. If your child goes on drop-off playdates, let his friend's parents know what your child can and can't watch.

routine. Unsure how to add a third person to their game, they resort to, "I don't want to be your friend" when they really mean, "We're busy right now. Can you come back in a few minutes?"

How to have fun with it

Mean or exclusionary behaviour often reflects a child's attempts to test boundaries and express feelings that aren't "allowed". Play games where he can exaggerate being mean. For example, let him be the super-strict teacher who gives you five time-outs or the mean big sister whose toys are off-limits. Sometimes you can use your child's enjoyment of testing boundaries by employing reverse psychology. Your child will get a kick out of it when you say in a stern voice, "Don't you dare put your toys away!" or "You better not eat your macaroni".

If your child announces to a peer in the playground, "You can't play!" don't shame him into engaging with that child; instead, gently redirect them to an activity they might enjoy

healthy play

The garden of eating

What you'll notice

Even if your child was a picky eater when she was a toddler, she may be more adventurous now. Younger children tend to be afraid of new foods, but by pre-school they have been exposed to lots of variety, so most edibles won't be scary. Additionally, research shows that children this age are heavily influenced by friends and imitate their eating habits when they're together. If her best friend gobbles up green beans, she probably will, too. Your pre-schooler will also eat more if she's had a hand in preparation or, better yet, if she planted and grew the fare herself. (And what 4-year-old doesn't love digging in the dirt?) A study of children at the University of California at Davis found that those who spent a year planting and tending to a vegetable garden not only knew more about nutrition, but ate significantly more veggies. If all you can accommodate is a tomato plant, start small but let your child do all of the caring and feeding of her windowsill garden.

Your child is starting to become adept at measuring and sorting so let her help prepare her own food.

Why it's happening

Curiosity and a desire to explore drive much of your child's behaviour, including her eating habits. Children this age love being in the kitchen – a largely adult domain – and by now are quite adept at stirring, pouring, and performing simple tasks like tearing lettuce for salad. They also love gadgets, so your child will be eager to get her hands on your eggbeater, apple corer – even your garlic press. Also intriguing to pre-schoolers is hearing how

the food they eat will affect their bodies. Play to your little one's desire to learn about her body and tell her that muscle-building protein will help her run faster, bone-building milk will help her grow taller, and brightly coloured veggies like carrots will keep her eyes sharp.

How to have fun with it

Invite your pint-size sous chef into the kitchen and pretend you're two chefs at a world-famous restaurant, or that you're preparing a meal for her favourite cartoon character. While supervised, she can use real utensils like a serrated knife (which is much more satisfying and effective than the dull plastic kind) and mix and pour to her delight. You can also provide your child with a few ingredients and challenge her to whip up her own delicious concoction.

At the supermarket, play "Who can find it first?" Give her a copy of your shopping list and see who can spot the items on the shelf first. Not only will this ward off shopping boredom, but it will also increase the chances that she'll want to eat her "finds". Let her choose a new fruit or veggie each week, then make a game of researching its background and preparing it when you get home.

Whenever possible, make mealtimes more enjoyable by setting the table, turning off the TV, and talking about your day. Numerous studies show that children who eat dinner with their families several nights per week do better academically and are less likely to engage in risky behaviour during the teen years. The good news is that your 4-year-old's longer attention span means she can actually sit still. That said, she'll probably only last about 10 minutes, so excuse her from the table when she's finished eating.

five-year-olds

Starting School

* * *

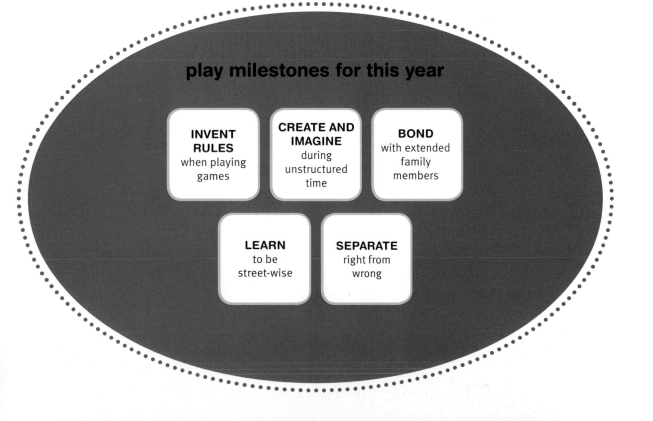

play milestones for this year

INVENT RULES
when playing games

CREATE AND IMAGINE
during unstructured time

BOND
with extended family members

LEARN
to be street-wise

SEPARATE
right from wrong

Starting School

You are officially out of the toddler and pre-school zones and poised to enter the world of big school. Thanks to huge strides in your 5-year-old's social and emotional growth, he not only understands appropriate behaviour, but actually craves structure and boundaries. Although he may suffer the occasional meltdown, he will weather minor upsets with relative calm, and the frenetic, frantic – and sometimes frustrating – behaviour of his younger days will give way to a more even temperament.

Your child's more grown-up demeanour, energy, and glass-half-full view of the world makes spending time with him a joy. Now that he speaks clearly, employing a vocabulary of over 1,500 words, and is able to express his feelings and ideas better, your conversations are rich with wacky insights, clever opinions, and uncensored observations. He still asks a lot of questions, but now he considers what he's asking more thoughtfully. Gone are the days of exasperating discipline. You may go hours – even days – without having to say, "No!" And when he digs in his heels or misbehaves, which he will, you can reason with him or explain what's upsetting you.

The bittersweet side of his increased maturity is that it signals a monumental new stage in his life: school. As he heads off to school, spending a full day or more in activities that you are no longer privy to, you face the challenge of accommodating a new and highly influential group of peers and other adults. Suddenly, his frame of reference shifts; through comparison and curiosity, he is figuring out who he is and where he came from, all of which can lead to a lot of questions about his extended family and personal history.

School also means lots of new rules and expectations that help him begin to separate right from wrong. Though he can show empathy for others and understands that other people have needs, too, he's not always able to put them before his own. His impulse control is still developing so he may break rules, brazenly cheat while playing a game, or exclaim "It's not fair!" when he doesn't get his way.

learning play

Right vs. wrong

What you'll notice

At 5, most children are in the early stages of developing a moral compass. Their ability to internalize the rules you've taught – to rely on their conscience – is still a couple of years off, so they look to you, other caregivers, and teachers to tell them the rules. Their struggle with learning to do the right thing comes through in their preoccupation with rules, fairness, good guys, and bad guys. Still very concrete in their thinking, 5-year-olds believe that what they want is what's "right", including winning at a game. Don't be surprised if, while playing a game, your child explains calmly how the rules have shifted in her favour.

Why it's happening

Doing the right thing requires the ability to control your impulses, take responsibility for your actions, and understand that what you do affects another person – all things that children this age have yet to master. Rules are especially hard to follow when a child experiences a desire to break them – grab a biscuit when Mum's back is turned, pocket a toy at a friend's house – or when she's tired or frustrated.

Experts believe that a 5-year-old's brain isn't physically capable of thinking abstractly or in a moral way; if no one sees her stealing the biscuit, chances are she won't feel guilty that

she's broken Mum's trust. Psychologists Jean Piaget and Lawrence Kohlberg, the forefathers in the field of children's moral development, discovered that 5-year-olds understand what rules are, but believe that they come from other people and that they're fixed and inflexible. Piaget's classic experiment was to tell young children stories about two children and to ask which child behaved worse: a child who breaks four cups while putting them away to surprise her mother or a child who accidentally breaks one cup while climbing onto the counter to get to off-limits sweets. Pre-schoolers and most 5-year-olds say that the child who broke four is more naughty because their concrete minds pay attention only to the number of cups broken, not to the children's intentions.

How to have fun with it

One of the best ways to teach children to follow the rules is to play board and card games that feature clear and simple steps and restrictions

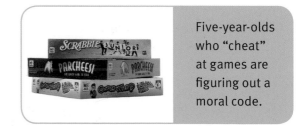

Five-year-olds who "cheat" at games are figuring out a moral code.

> We try to involve our kids in the rule-making so that they feel more control over and more committed to following the rules (such as, 'one piece of cake for dessert when you finish dinner'). It works – sometimes!
>
> — Eliza, mother of three

or consequences. Outdoor games like tag or "Piggy in the Middle" move quickly and the "winner" changes often enough to keep your impulsive player in line. When your child tries to make up her own rules ("I get to move my piece ahead of yours because it's red" or "My card wins because it's older"), ask if she wants to start the game over so you can both play by these new rules. It's likely that she'll prefer to stick with the game at hand.

When she remembers a rule on her own and follows it, point out what you liked about her behaviour during the game: "You did really well following the rules and waiting for your go to move!"

When it comes to rules and routines, consistency is key. Children who learn early on that we tidy up our toys, wear a helmet while bike riding, and always buckle our seatbelts don't have to be nagged or cajoled into following the rules. Just be sure to stick to your own code of conduct, because the axiom,

"Do as I do, not as I say", applies big-time at this age. When your child inevitably breaks a rule, try to remain calm; losing your temper and yelling may scare her so much that she'll hesitate to tell you the truth in the future.

learning play

The benefits of boredom

What you'll notice

If your child was enrolled in a pre-school programme last year, it would have taken up just a fraction of his time. Now that he's in Year 1, he spends at least half his day in the classroom, making new friends he's eager to see outside of school. On top of that he may have after-school activities that can quickly turn his schedule into a fast-paced dash from one place to another. As exciting and fun as his busy life may be, he probably has little downtime and few opportunities to just sit with his thoughts, exercising his fertile imagination.

Why it's happening

Daydreaming and navel-gazing may seem like a waste of time, especially when your friends are signing up their 5-year-olds for football club, music classes, and tae kwon do. But child psychology experts believe that downtime has huge benefits for your young child's cognitive and emotional growth. Unscheduled and unrushed time – plain old boredom – encourages your child to invent, create, and explore his interests at his own pace. Solo imaginary play, which requires him to structure his own fun, has long-term pay-offs. Researchers at Case Western Reserve University in Cleveland found that children whose play included emotion and fantasy were more creative and better able to problem-solve and cope with stress.

Boredom also teaches your child that just sitting still and doing nothing can be extremely rewarding. He can create stories in his mind, think through problems and, importantly, learn to be alone with his thoughts and feelings, a skill that will benefit him throughout his life.

How to have fun with it

When you hear the dreaded refrain, "I'm bored", don't rush in to entertain and resist the urge to turn on the TV or computer. Instead, provide open-ended materials such as art supplies and dressing-up clothes. If your child has difficulty with undirected time, set a manageable goal

Provide art supplies for those "nothing-to-do" moments.

Did you know?

Turning off the TV and eliminating extraneous activities will do more than increase your child's daydreaming hours. He's likely to dream more at night, because he will get more shut-eye. According to several studies, overscheduling, high-tech entertainment, and other diversions have robbed children today of about one hour of sleep per night, compared to thirty years ago.

Daydreaming may never make it onto your to-do list and, in our fast-paced lives, "vegging out" gets a bad rap, but scheduling downtime can help you as much as it helps your child. Our children learn from our example, so turn off the screens and teach your child that it's okay to do nothing. Better yet, keep him company when he's lying on the lawn; cuddle together to watch the sunset; or take an aimless walk in the woods.

– say, ten minutes – and then gradually extend his solo time. At first, you may need to point out examples of things he can do, but chances are you'll be floored by his creativity and imagination in the face of boredom.

Set up and suggest some nice, quiet spots for daydreaming. This can be a cozy chair by a window, a hammock, a tent in the house or garden, or just a blanket on the living room floor. You can also teach your child to close his eyes and simply follow his breath or you can introduce simple relaxation techniques such as tensing and relaxing each part of his body. Yoga is another good option, since children this age have the physical flexibility to hold the poses.

Most importantly, leave your child alone when he's really engrossed in something. Experts call this "flow", being so totally wrapped up in what you're doing that you lose track of time. This state of mind is a very satisfying place, so try not to interrupt, even if that occasionally means skipping a bath.

loving play

Family ties

What you'll notice

When you tell stories about your childhood, your child is fully engaged. She asks questions about relatives and loves looking at old family photos and movies – especially those in which she's the leading lady. In fact, she'll be happy to point out, "There's me!" every time she recognizes herself on the screen.

If you have a blended family, your child may have a better understanding of how the two families came together and ask questions about step-relatives. An adopted child may suddenly want to know more about her birth parents – even if you've described the lucky day you found her countless times before. And if you haven't broached the subject of her adoption, this is the time to explore ways to introduce it.

Because children this age hear a lot about their pals' home lives, you may learn that "Mia has two houses because her mum and dad don't live together", or "Jason doesn't have a dad". If your child has grandparents, her time with them will be even more special than when she was younger, a feeling that's probably mutual.

Why it's happening

As an infant, toddler, and even a pre-schooler, your child's view of the world was primarily a self-centred one. Having now ventured out into school and other social arenas, she compares herself to others, sparking an appetite to learn more about her family and personal history.

How to have fun with it

There are myriad ways to help your child connect with her personal history. Use photos to create a timeline or family tree, or put together a scrapbook about your family. Interviewing relatives is another way she can unearth some interesting information. If relatives are too far away for a face-to-face meeting, help your child come up with a few interview questions, then email or post them to your relatives. Put the responses in a folder and create a family history book that she'll love looking at again and again. You and your child can also research the country where your ancestors came from, or if she was adopted, where she was born.

Encourage your child's relationships with

With a camera of her own, your child can send photos to far-away relatives.

Homemade fun

Many adults find it rewarding to establish a special ritual with a niece, nephew, or godchild. It could be as simple as making biscuits or playing draughts. The value for kids and adults alike is the bond the ritual creates.

her relatives, scheduling visits and keeping in touch. Many studies suggest that the more caring adults your child has in her life, the better off she'll be. Other studies indicate that children who are close to their grandparents have a stronger sense of family, achieve better in school, and may even steer clear of future trouble like drugs and violence. Allow your child to develop special activities and routines that she does only with her grandparents or other close relatives such as playing chess, going fishing, or collecting old coins. Unencumbered by the day-to-day details of a child's life, grandparents tend to have the patience to teach new skills, and their unconditional love is a blessing in any child's life.

Even a child who lives far from her grandparents or relatives can build a bond. Modern technology makes it possible to do everything from talking on the phone (which 5-year-olds love) to playing a game like "20 questions" with Grandma via a webcam or video conference. Your child will also love making pictures and presents for far-flung relatives – especially if she sees a photo of her artwork hanging on their refrigerator. Before spending time with relatives that you

don't see often, hang up their photos and tell your child stories about them. If your child is familiar with their faces, she's likely to be more comfortable when she sees them in person.

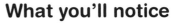

healthy play

Kicking the habit

What you'll notice

Spend a morning in the classroom and chances are you'll see plenty of nail biting, thumb sucking, hair twirling, and nose picking. Amazingly, children this age engage in these self-soothing habits with the same lack of self-consciousness or embarrassment that they bring to other aspects of their life. Engrossed in a story or tired from breaktime, they revert to behaviours that often involve their mouths – a throwback to babyhood.

Why it's happening

Life as a 5-year-old seems pretty carefree, but even the most easy-going child can have a hard time transitioning from pre-school to Year 1. Though excited, she also feels a bit ambivalent about being such a big kid and might seek solace by sucking her thumb or chewing her collar. Another reason for these habits, according to some studies, is that they may help your child concentrate and stay alert. Or she may be copying the behaviour of an adult or older sibling.

How to have fun with it

Nail biting can be the hardest habit to break, which is why an estimated 20 per cent of kids who nibble now will still do so as adults. Gnawed nails not only look bad, they're unhealthy. Tearing up the protective skin around the nail bed invites infection-causing bacteria into the body. Most children who bite their nails or suck their thumb don't usually wash their hands before doing so, which means they're putting germs in their mouth many times a day. Many of these problems will go away on their own thanks to peer pressure. It is likely that the first time a classmate tells your child how gross it is that she bites her nails or picks her nose, she'll stop.

In the meantime, keep little hands busy by giving her a small toy, fabric scrap, or modelling clay to put in her pocket and fidget or fiddle with when the urge hits.

Keeping hands busy with clay or small toys can distract a thumbsucker or nail-biter.

Playing it safe

Pause before you paint your child's thumbs with nasty-tasting products, which often fail to cure a thumb-sucker's habit and can occasionally cause stomach aches. And always check with your doctor first before trying any "homemade" cure.

Get to the root of the problem by keeping a log of when these habits happen such as "before football practice" or "after school". In a week or so you may see a pattern in situations when she's stressed, tired, or upset. If anxiety is the cause, teach your child healthier ways to calm down like deep breathing, relaxation techniques, and yoga.

Thumb sucking shouldn't be as bothersome as the other habits since most children outgrow this on their own. Forty-five per cent of 2-year-olds suck their thumbs while only 5 per cent of 11-year-olds do the same. Also, as long as she kicks the habit before her permanent teeth come in, your thumbsucker isn't destined to rack up the orthodonture bills.

Reading is a terrific way to help your child avoid bad habits, as many children's books address these subjects. You can also try rewarding your child with stickers for going long periods without engaging in a nasty habit. (Experts say it takes 28 days to form a new more positive habit.)

The street-wise kid

What you'll notice

This year, your child ventures further afield than he has in the past. Though still under your watchful eye, he spends more time biking up and down the driveway or pavement, playing in the garden, and enjoying time at the park and playground. Because he's old enough, you can visit places like amusement parks and arcades, child-friendly museums and art galleries, and beaches – all of them rich in distractions.

Five-year-olds tend to be very friendly and at ease, even with people they don't know. They're eager to make friends and love showing off. At the same time, they're still extremely curious and have a hard time controlling their impulses, which can make them vulnerable to temptations.

Why it's happening

Times have changed since you were a 5-year-old playing in the garden until dark while your parents were inside. Most of us have seen the scary headlines about children abducted or the footage of a child being lured off the playground by a person with a cute puppy. The "don't talk to strangers" rule that you were taught as a child doesn't apply anymore either.

In fact, ask a 5-year-old what a stranger is and he'll probably describe a mean-looking person whom he's never met before. Unfortunately, it's not just the scary-looking people or those we don't know who harm children. Plus, adults often contradict this rule when we chat with the attendants at the coffee shop or garage. That said, you shouldn't deprive your child of the joys of being a kid and engaging in carefree play. You simply have to keep your eye on him and give him some tools and rules to help keep him safe.

How to have fun with it

This is an age where your child is good at following rules (or at least interested in proving that he can), so it's actually possible to teach him what to do if he's in trouble; for example, if he becomes separated from you in public.

Give your child a whistle so he can blow on it loudly if you are separated in public.

Through pretend play, you can explain that he should stay where he is and wait for you to come to him. You can also explain that, if he's lost, it's best to ask a mum with kids or another woman for help. You can also stress that he never take anything from strangers; never walk near parked cars or get into a car with someone he doesn't know; and be wary of an adult asking for help or directions. Teach your child that if a stranger says, "Don't shout", he should do the opposite.

Games like Freeze Tag or "Red Light, Green Light" help your child practise what it's like to stop and wait. You can also present "What if?" scenarios. For example, "What would you do if a grown up you didn't know asked you for help?" His answers provide a jumping-off point for a conversation about safety.

Another game you can play is "What did you see?" After you come home from a walk or a drive, ask him questions about where you were. Did you see that man with the blue shirt? How many children did we see? Were there people walking in front of us? Doing this regularly trains your child to take note of his environment and to stay alert.

Lastly, teach him his home phone or your mobile phone number and his address. Tuck a piece of paper with this information in his shoe (under the insole) or in a jacket pocket.

six-year-olds
Energy and Adventures

* * *

play milestones for this year

READ independently

COLLECT dinosaurs, dolls, etc.

RIDE bike without training wheels

DEVELOP COMPASSION

OVERCOME SHYNESS

MAKE DECISIONS independently

WRITE upper- and lower-case

Energy and Adventures

For parents raising primary school children, this year is full of surprises. Your child wows everyone with her sincerity, intensity, and willingness to throw herself headfirst into all kinds of new interests. Whether it's football, stamp collecting, or dinosaurs, her passions are both fierce and fleeting.

All that energy can create an unruly package, and many parents worry about the constant fidgeting that so often appears during these years. Foot tapping, chair jiggling, and jumping up and down from the dinner table are typical. In fact, this is an age when lots of parents begin to wonder if their child may have attention problems. Experts say, however, as long as your 6-year-old can focus on a project for about 15 minutes, she's right where she should be.

Sudden growth spurts can make your child clumsy, and in some children, those gangly looks (and missing teeth) can create a bit of an Ugly Duckling phase. Like the duckling, your child is blossoming. Every day, she may come home from school and seem like a new person. "I hate chunky peanut butter," she'll declare, "and I love strawberry milk." You'll think, "Really? Since when?" Or she'll announce a desire to learn the drums or to wear only short-sleeved shirts.

Adding to that "Who is this child, and where did she come from?" feeling, many parents get another insight at the beginning of primary school, the first glimpse that peers and other adults see your child very differently to how you do. It's often astonishing to parents to find that their tantrum-prone only child is famous for her great turn-taking skills at break time, or that others regard their shy little girl as the most sought-after snack-time companion.

For many parents, these realizations are bittersweet. Your child is probably telling you less than she did last year about her life at school and she may also show a new streak of self-criticism ("I'm the worst speller in the whole world!") and a wobbly sense of self-esteem. Moods can be volatile, and your child may start withdrawing from adults and focusing more on peers. Even though it's exciting to watch her interests and skills start to expand, it's hard not to feel a little shut out at times.

Six-year-olds often display a pseudo-adult charm. And in many ways, they are much more grown-up in their thinking: children this age can now distinguish between fantasy and reality, and quickly make connections and distinctions between feelings, thoughts, and actions. Not only are they adept at identifying problems, they're delighted to solve them, and they exude a new spirit of pluck and mastery. "Look," your son might say, proudly carrying in a plate, "I made myself a sausage-and-ketchup sandwich, and I made one for you, too!" Enjoy every bite!

learning play

Ready, set, read!

What you'll notice

Of all the breakthroughs you've been noticing so far, from first steps to first words, learning to read ranks as one of the most thrilling – and most gratifying. But the years-long process that takes your child from board to chapter books is a complex journey, one that entails much more than letters on a page.

The European Academy of Paediatrics says that by the age of 6 or 7, most children are reading. They not only master easy "sight" words, like "cat" and "ball", but use phonics to sound out words they've never seen before, usually with great *per-se-ver-ance*. And they use little tricks that quickly become second nature, like looking for a word's context or synonyms.

Why it's happening

Your child's passion for reading now connects significantly to other emerging skills. For example, reading boosts empathy: actively trying to understand how another person feels allows your new reader to put himself in a character's shoes. Researchers have even noticed an increase in empathy when children are asked to imagine the point of view of an animal, plant, or inanimate object. Conversely, empathy boosts reading. While most younger children can't understand the idea of a narrator, 6-year-olds, who are able to take on a different

perspective, grasp the concept easily. They can even follow complicated stories where the narrator shifts.

How to have fun with it

Incorporate words and language into as many games and activities as possible. Or dedicate a day to a letter and have milk, macaroni, and meatballs for your meal on Monday. And all children love a treasure hunt that includes deciphering the clues you can write in Dr Seuss style rhymes: "For Clue Three, look near the TV".

According to a study conducted by children's book publisher Scholastic and the research firm Yankelovich, 92 per cent of children this age say books are fun, and 40 per cent say they read every day. But by the time kids turn 8, they begin to read less and less. As tempting as it is to blame computers, researchers found that pint-sized techies are likely to read for fun. Television, on the other hand, does cut into

A doll or game based on a book's favourite character will strengthen your child's connection to the text.

Homemade fun

At school, your child probably has a "word wall", which can inspire similar fun at home. Take turns attaching sticky notes to things around the house, from easy ones ("rug") to the exotic ("chaise longue").

reading time, according to a study from the University of Texas at Austin and Harvard Children's Hospital, so limit TV and video time to no more than two hours per day.

There are lots of ways to make sure your child enjoys reading for years to come. A critical part, experts say, is that your child has access to all kinds of books, from easy-readers to more in-depth books about their passions. Make a stop at a bookstore or local library part of your weekly routine, and encourage reluctant readers with comics and joke books.

At home, make sure his room has a cozy corner for reading, with a comfy place to sit, a good lamp, and a bookcase, so he can learn to read in private. But even when he can read proficiently on his own, don't stop reading to him. Not only is listening to stories a great way to boost your child's reading skills, it reminds him that reading is one of life's great pleasures, a way for families to share memories, laughs, and high drama, whether it's courtesy of J.K. Rowling, Hans Christian Andersen, or Jacqueline Wilson. Most importantly, talk about books and read as much as possible yourself. According to the Yankelovich research, children of high-frequency readers were much more likely to read for fun than other kids.

learning play

Instilling values that last

What you'll notice

All parents want to raise good children who live their lives according to certain values. But at this age, your child may frequently say or do things you don't like. She may cheat when she plays games or whine that certain rules just aren't fair. Some days, she may be great at sharing; the next, she refuses to take turns. She may be incredibly tender and kind with one friend, then turn around and stick her tongue out at another. And it doesn't help that the TV programmes she seems drawn to favour smart-alecky humour and sarcasm that send messages contrary to your family's values.

Why it's happening

Your child is struggling to learn right from wrong, whether that applies to the rules of Uno or playground etiquette. While she's still several years away from a more fully developed conscience, she is eager to please her parents and other adults. She wants to do the right thing, and often, she even knows what that is. It's just still a bit of a struggle for her to fight the strong impulses to win every game, or to get what she wants right this minute.

> " Every spring, we clean out the children's bedrooms and collect all of the toys and books they've outgrown. Whatever is in good condition we take to a children's hospital or homeless shelter.
> – Doug, father of two "

At 6, children see the value of donating money to a good cause they deem worthy.

animals, but it means more if she gives a little of her pocket money to a local animal shelter.

Look for local organizations that welcome younger volunteers. If such opportunities are scarce, help kids organize small fundraisers, such as car boot sales and lemonade stands, so they can donate cash to local programmes.

How to have fun with it

Start by deciding what values you want to teach. In some families, being thrifty and taking care of older relatives may top the list. In others, protecting the environment or helping people who have less may be paramount. Not sure what matters most? Some teachers suggest involving the children in writing a simple mission statement. Even something as basic as, "We believe in treating others as we would like to be treated, helping others, and taking good care of animals and the planet", will help you focus on the values that mean the most to you.

Then act consistently on those values in concrete ways. "Helping others" is vague; taking Great-Aunt Mary her groceries every other week is concrete. And since 6-year-olds tend to get very excited about group projects, talk to your child's teacher about involving the class. Some schools, for example, set up a table in the cafeteria where children can bring food donations for local charities.

Two goals, experts say, are cultivating senses of gratitude and responsibility. It's important for children to be able to count their blessings and to share those blessings with others. It's fine to love

Decisions, decisions

What you'll notice

At 6, your child is eager to try everything at once. A friend comes over to play, and the next thing you know they have dragged every single game and costume out of the cupboard. When it's time to get dressed in the morning, she may deliberate for a very long time about which pair of leggings to wear. As indecisive as she seems, she's also developing skills that enable her to make thoughtful decisions.

Why this is happening

While she's still a few years away from the level of reasoning that will allow her to make rational decisions, she is willing to take on problems in a new way, and with her longer attention span, she is better equipped to weigh multiple possibilities against one another. Experts have found that when children this age are taught to solve problems on their own, rather than having adults settle conflicts for them, those critical skills follow them well into later life.

How to have fun with it

Recognizing that Year 2 children are able to make decisions – individually and as a group – schools often incorporate something called social decision-making into daily routines. The class may decide together, for example, how they should tackle their new material on penguins, or even how they should structure their day: music first, then maths, or vice versa?

You can encourage the same thing at home: "Do you want to do your spelling homework first or your reading? Why?" "Should we have pork chops or pasta?" Many of the things we do are simply arbitrary, but it's fun to practise her reasoning skills. ("Reading first, because this

> "To give my son a little control over his decisions and help him learn from his mistakes, I try to step back when he orders an unusual ice cream flavour I think he may regret."
> – Ursula, mother of one

worksheet will be boring. We already had pasta this week, so I'd rather have pork chops.")

Teach her the ancient art of the "pro" and "con" list, and extend the process to family decisions. Let's say the problem is planning Saturday afternoon. Your child wants to go to the park, and you've got to buy the week's food shopping. Get her to dictate the pros of doing what she wants first (the earlier in the day you go to the park, the warmer it will be) versus the cons (the supermarket will be crowded later on) and then review your list together.

Or if she and her brother are wrestling over the remote, insist they come up with different sharing scenarios. This can make your family closer, giving everyone the chance to voice an opinion. Of course, your child won't be thrilled when she's overruled, but at least she will feel heard. She will also learn that most decisions involve some type of compromise. Finally, look for games that encourage deductive reasoning, like the classic guessing game "Guess Who?"

Games like draughts help a child to weigh up decisions before taking her turn.

loving play

Introvert or extrovert?

What you'll notice

By now, you should have a sense of your child's basic personality type: about 25 to 30 per cent of children are very outgoing, and 15 to 20 per cent are quite shy, personality researchers have found. Watching shy children struggle at school and in social situations is hard, and knowing your child feels excluded from playground games and lunchtime cliques can sting.

Although extroverted kids seem to have an easier time – moving through any crowd, making new friends, and greeting old ones filled of enthusiasm – they can find it difficult to spend time alone.

Why it's happening

Your child isn't becoming more or less extroverted because of school, although it can seem that way. He's probably been that way since birth: research on identical twins and other genetic studies have shown that a tendency toward extroversion, introversion, and shyness is highly hereditary. But now that he's

Did you know?

Women who conceive in August or September are more likely to have a shy child nine months later, according to researchers at Harvard. Early autumns's diminishing daylight causes Mum's body to produce more melatonin, which passes through the placenta. The developing brain is exposed to this hormone, which may act on the baby's cells to create the temperament associated with shyness.

moving among so many more children, his temperament, particularly if he falls at either end of the social spectrum, may strike you as problematic. But there's a difference between being an introvert – which is approximately 30 per cent of the population – and being shy. Children in the latter group, which makes up about 15 to 20 per cent of kids, are afraid of people. Introverts just prefer to be alone.

How to have fun with it

Pushing a shy child into more social interactions than he wants – or asking that his teacher do so – is not wise. For the sake of his own confidence, he needs to learn to do this on his own; besides, such efforts often backfire. As much as parents would like to believe primary school is just like pre-school, it's not. Two 6-year-olds can't be forced to have fun together in the same way that younger children can. Most importantly, because shyness is largely genetic, trying to affect a child's basic

temperament won't work and may undermine your relationship. At 6, he will sense that the "shy" label has negative connotations or, worse, that you think there's something fundamentally wrong with him. You can help, though. If your child comes home from school talking about someone new, suggest he initiate a playdate: children usually choose friends with similar interests and temperaments. And let him know that you can see that playing with other kids is difficult for him. Give him plenty of time to rest before a party, for example, and let him know that leaving early is an option.

Role-playing games help, too. "First, I'll ask you to play a game. Then you think of a game you can ask me to play." And when he does have a friend over, have a few games and activities planned to keep things moving.

When you're out together, model the behaviours you would like your child to feel more comfortable doing – saying "Hello" or shaking hands. Most importantly, if you were (or are) shy, talk about how it feels to get past your anxiety: "I was a little nervous introducing myself to Mrs Jones, but she was so nice, I'm glad I did it."

Designing a paper doll can help a child express her personality.

loving play

Raising caring children

What you'll notice

Watching children this age at play can be hard. They seem to exhibit no loyalty, moving from group to group, bestowing the distinction of "best friend" at random, and telling tales on their siblings or peers. They tend to be sore losers, often flinging game pieces across the room in frustration.

They are also highly sensitive, exclaiming, "You hurt my feelings", or sulking when scolded. This sensitivity extends to others. When a pal is upset, your 6-year-old may try to comfort her or find an adult to help out. Listening to a sad story, she may get teary or get angry that the book made her sad. And when she experiences strong emotions herself or on behalf of others, she'll have lots of questions: "Why did Sylvie say I can't play?"

Why it's happening

Compassion doesn't develop overnight. Researchers have seen acts of extreme compassion in children as young as 21 months, and it's a trait that we continue to refine well into adulthood. But this year – with your child's rapidly enlarging social sphere – there are nonstop opportunities to learn caring behaviour.

How to have fun with it

You can encourage tolerance and empathy by making sure your child gets plenty of time to play in environments with a large mix of people. Parks and playgrounds where young and old, affluent and poor, and people of different ethnicities mingle naturally expose children to a variety of cultures and characters.

You can also encourage your child to become a student of the world by researching online other countries, languages, costumes, and games. Try new ethnic foods, start a foreign coin collection, or consider sponsoring a child in another country. Often these groups supply pictures and accounts of daily life that will captivate your child as she learns to

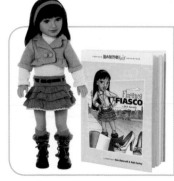

Dolls and books about other cultures help children gain a sense of tolerance.

Did you know?

Getting into the habit of volunteering now pays off later. Children who are raised to care for others – specifically by volunteering – reap the benefits themselves later. Teens who are active volunteers are 50 per cent less likely to engage in destructive behaviour or to abuse drugs, alcohol, or cigarettes, reports the U.S. Bureau of Statistics.

identify the ways in which she is the same and very different from her far-flung "pal". Some television programs can assist in teaching your child compassion: according to a study by the National Institute of Mental Health, children tend to imitate the kindness they see on television, so look for shows and characters that encourage children to be open-minded and helpful. Conversely, if you see something together that is mean or bigoted, take advantage of this moment to ask your child what she thinks, then share your thoughts.

Most of all, experts say, try and set an example yourself. Whether it's helping out lonely neighbours, offering a kind word to a homeless person, or going out of your way to cheer up a sick friend, share these small acts of kindness with your child.

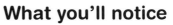

healthy play

The write stuff

What you'll notice

As you watch your child's writing become more controlled and deliberate, it's fun to see him tackling new projects, from letters to the Tooth Fairy to his first diary. Good handwriting takes lots of practice, and he'll get plenty in school. Throughout Key Stage One, the emphasis is likely to be on upper and lower case printing; towards the end of Year 2, some teachers begin to introduce the basics of cursive writing.

Why it's happening

Children learn to write in stages: when they're little, they grab a crayon with all four fingers and their thumb, clutching it. Next, they move on to a palm-down position. But by age 6, the majority of children have enough fine motor skills to employ the classic tripod grip, using their middle finger, index finger, and thumb to

> " My son and I love to make lists together. He does the writing. The themes are fun: his favourite sports stars, my favourite foods, our favourite songs. It sparks conversation and he gets writing practice. "
>
> – Roberta, mother of two

balance the pencil. (The majority of adults write this way – 88 per cent, in fact.)

How to have fun with it

You can help at home by watching the way your child writes. Experts say most children settle into their own flow, but some habitually hold their pencil the wrong way, developing clumsy and even painful writing styles. (Holding the pen too tightly is the most common problem, or tucking the thumb under the other fingers.) If he seems to be struggling, the triangular shaped grips sold at office-supply shops may help. And make sure he has a settled place to do his writing: he needs a chair where his feet can reach the floor, and a flat, child-sized table or desk. Keep other art supplies in the area, too, since his new fine-motor coordination are likely to inspire him to draw and paint.

To make writing inviting, keep plenty of bright writing paper, fun pens, pencils, and fine-tipped markers around, so he can write on his own. Buy him a special notebook, so he can jot down his thoughts and activities, and give him a notepad on holidays, so he can write a travel journal. Let your child be in charge of

writing things down on the family calendar, shopping lists, and thank-you notes.

There are other ways to boost fine-motor control. Pick-Up Sticks and "Rock, Paper, Scissors" are fun games. And many crafts – braiding, lacing, and using tweezers to pick up beads or stones – will let him flex his creativity while strengthening his fingers. Let him help you in the kitchen by shelling peas or placing little decorations on iced cupcakes.

In case you're wondering, he won't be switching hands. Experts used to believe children's handedness stabilized during the early school years, but researchers at Queen's University in Belfast have shown that most of us establish our left- or right-handed preference in utero.

Beads and other toys that work small finger muscles indirectly help kids develop writing skills.

seven-year-olds

The Sweet and Savvy Stage

* * *

play milestones for this year

DECLARE A BEST FRIEND

ADD AND SUBTRACT easily

PLAY A MUSICAL instrument

JOIN a team

DEVELOP GOOD MANNERS

BECOME CURIOUS about sex

MOVE IN TIME to a beat

HANDLE CONFLICT on their own

The Sweet and Savvy Stage

It makes sense that 7-year-olds love riddles; almost everything about this year is a paradox. On one hand, your Year 3 child still has a close personal relationship with the Tooth Fairy; on the other, she wakes up singing a Gwen Stefani song. She can be a loving, loyal friend, yet turn around and invent a club that excludes the girl she seemed to worship last week. She can be a relentless "researcher", demanding an explanation of exactly how an engine creates a spark, and then ask to be picked up and cuddled "like when I was little".

It's also a year of fast-paced learning and intellectual growth. Not only is she reading fairly well, she's priming her brain for a lifetime of literacy. Researchers at the University of Zurich have found that certain patterns of neurons, required to recognize the long strings of print needed for reading, peak at this age. The charming invented spellings of the earlier years start to fade away; instead, your 7-year-old proudly shows you sentences that are neater, with capital letters, correct punctuation, maybe even some cursive script.

And there are plenty of practical breakthroughs. Your child can tell the time and count money. Simple consequences begin to make sense to her. She may understand – without prompting – that if she dawdles at breakfast, she'll miss the bus. She's resourceful, and prone to answering her own questions; for example, "What does this word mean?" with "I could look it up in the dictionary."

Her emotional growth is also rapid; you'll notice a greater ability to describe what's going on around her, and how she feels about it. She's learning how to control herself, and may surprise you with her insights: "I'm so frustrated with this homework! I think I'll feel better if I finish it in my room."

But perhaps the biggest leaps happen on the playground, as she learns to navigate the world of her peers. Previously easy-going play relationships are replaced by cliques; yesterday's best buddy is today's tormentor. Above all, she wants to fit in, and anything that makes her stand out – from the wrong bookbag to a new haircut – may make her uneasy. Still, she's increasingly ready to join in the game – any game. This is the age when she will probably want to join the netball or swimming team. For her, sports aren't just a great way to exercise; they represent a whole new arena for social development and a way to become comfortable with her growing body.

learning play

Creative challenges

What you'll notice

In some ways, you can see that your child is pouring more of himself into his creative activities – injecting real feeling and rhythm into the way he dances, for instance, or using subtle new brush techniques in his watercolour rainforests. What's more, he appreciates true creativity in others. He can sit, completely spellbound, through longer performances or articulate a strong opinion about a film or book.

But you'll also notice something a little disappointing: when it comes to his work at school, he may seem to be less creative, as if he's striving to make his paintings, drawings, and stories less imaginative and more like all the other children's. In the same way, he'll want to choose play activities not so much because he enjoys them, but because "everyone else is doing it".

Why it's happening

Creativity in children starts to decline at this age, and will do so for the next several years, hitting its lowest point at around age 10. (Psychologists even refer to this trend as the Year 6 slump.) Don't worry – your child isn't turning into a total conformist. Experts say that his newfound interest in peers and his growing self-consciousness make him far less willing to take creative risks. Learning how to fit in, he doesn't want to do anything that might make him stand out.

How to have fun with it

Remember, your child's creativity is as much a function of what he absorbs as what he produces. Now is a wonderful time to expose him to all kinds of art – from trips to museums and galleries to local concerts and dance performances. Many organizations offer child-friendly beginners' classes in everything from comedy improvization to dance to classical guitar, and if your child seems interested, by all means, sign him up.

Seven-year-olds love to learn about how others poured their heart and soul into art,

> " When I take my daughter to a museum, we stop at the gift shop first to buy postcards of some of the paintings and then see who can spot them first. Or we play categories, counting how many birds or angels we spot in a work of art!
> – Carl, father of one "

whether it's Louis Armstrong or Pablo Picasso. Just as your child is learning to recognize musical ideas like tempo, rhythm and tone, he's learning to articulate how that makes him feel. In visual arts, children this age are especially drawn to abstract pieces, and often like to experiment with creating it on their own. (In making abstract art, they don't have to worry about whether it's "right" or not.)

If your child is stifling his creative impulses at school in order to conform to the tastes of his peers, provide plenty of opportunities for creative play at home, setting up an easel in a more secluded part of the house, and respecting his desire to work in private. Or work on a craft project together where there is no "right" way for it to come out, like tie-dyeing tee shirts.

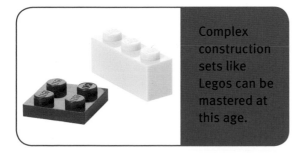

Complex construction sets like Legos can be mastered at this age.

learning play

First finances

What you'll notice

As your child becomes more and more curious about how adults function in the world, she asks questions about grown-up stuff: "How does the cash point know not to give our money to someone else? Can I buy a motorcycle with my tooth money? Are we rich?" Because she can add and subtract now, she's more likely to pay attention to your transactions, and may even ask if she can count your change in shops.

Why it's happening

In many ways, your 7-year-old's sudden interest in money is rooted in maths. Not only is she learning the value of each coin, but many of the lessons she's studying at school focus on the number 100 – a natural bridge to the pound. Her interest in high finance also reflects her observations of what makes the world go 'round. Money, at least to her eyes, equals independence. It's what enables people to buy toys, ride on trains, and go to restaurants. And it's obvious that some people have more than others, an inequity that may rankle her burgeoning sense of ethics. She also notices how her "stuff" measures up against that of her peers. Suddenly, having a name-brand shirt or owning the latest gadget can take on greater importance.

How to have fun with it

Right now, despite her increasing awareness of what other children are up to, she relies on your opinions and values to guide her. Even if she seems obsessed with the cost of things or seems to have a bad case of the "gimmes", she wants to learn, not just bargain for more stuff.

The best way to teach children about money, says the American Academy of Pediatrics, is to let them have access to some of their own. Start by laying out the rules, providing a context for how much she can spend and on what. Some parents are adamant that children not be paid to do chores, others encourage it. Some think a weekly allowance, often in the amount of 50 pence per year of the child's age, is a great idea; others believe it's best to just respond to a child's requests at the moment.

Experts say the details aren't important, as long as families are consistent and explain their

A bank of one's own encourages saving up for something special.

Homemade fun

Deputize your child as the family coin officer, rounding up change she finds in sofa cushions, on cupboard floors, or in the laundry room. Keep a ledger so she can track her finds and see how change adds up (and let her keep a portion of each week's haul).

reasoning and values to their kids. If you're at the supermarket and your child asks for a toy you think is a piece of junk, don't say, "I don't have enough money to buy that" unless that's really the reason. Instead, tell the truth: "I don't think that toy is well-made and I don't want to waste money on it."

It's also important to teach children to set aside a portion of their cash for spending, for charity, and for saving. You can use envelopes, but many kids like see-through containers, like jars or clear piggy banks, so they can watch their coins accumulate. At this age, kids have a very limited sense of what "the future" means, so help your child set very short-term savings goals; maybe there's a toy or book she can save up to buy in a few weeks. You can help her stay on track by not giving her money when she runs out.

All children benefit from giving to others, either as part of their family's charitable efforts, through school fundraising efforts, or as part of their spiritual practice. Research shows that children often get more than they give in terms of self-esteem, confidence, and gratitude.

loving play

Best friends, worst enemies

What you'll notice

Seven-year-olds form and dissolve alliances so fast your head may spin with each update: "Ashley is my new best friend", your child announces at breakfast, only to come home sobbing, "Ashley says Maya is her new best friend, and they wouldn't let me sit with them at lunch!"

Cliques, teasing, and bullying are ubiquitous at this age: a recent study found that nine out of ten secondary school students have been bullied by their peers in the past year, and six in ten children have participated in some type of bullying themselves. Girls tend to use what experts call social aggression: "Let's start a club and not let Amanda join!" Boys tend to be more physically aggressive. And disturbing as it is, children are also using the Internet to be cruel, especially in chat rooms and via Instant Messaging.

> "I often organize activity-based playdates so my daughter and her friends don't end up holed up in her bedroom talking about other children. I'll take them ice skating or to the park. I give them their privacy but keep them engaged in something healthy.
>
> — Angela, mother of two

Why it's happening

Children this age are increasingly self-conscious and insecure about their standing socially, so they form cliques in order to belong. But the whole point of a clique is to make someone feel left out – even if that child was everybody's favourite the day before. Mostly, this fluid social aggression affects every child at some point, but it can also progress to more intense bullying, with certain children being constantly ostracized. And just because it's common doesn't mean it's harmless. Children who get picked on frequently have been shown to develop serious adjustment problems, and in some cases, even depression, so do not wait to step in. But 7-year-olds are also learning to be good friends, drawing on their growing reservoir of compassion and empathy.

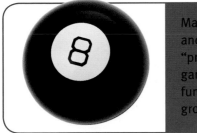

Magic 8-Balls and other "prediction" games are fun for small groups.

How to have fun with it

While there's nothing fun about cliques or bullying, children this age find myriad ways to support and love one another. If your child has a BFF, make sure you support that (even if she's not your favourite person in the whole world), helping your child organize the sleepovers and giggle fests that make relationships special.

Tell her stories about your own childhood: the fact that someone called you "four-eyes" and that you cried, too, may be comforting. At the same time, try to get her thinking about what motivates others to be mean; she will probably quickly recognize that children shun others just to feel part of the crowd, and she may even empathize with their need to do so.

Even if your child doesn't seem to have any problems with cliques in school, introduce her to activities that may provide different sources of friends – gymnastics lessons, Scouts, or a youth group associated with your place of worship. That way, when she does get the cold shoulder at school (psychologists say only 15 per cent of children can be described as popular, which means 85 per cent are struggling in the lower social echelons), she'll have other friends on whom she can rely.

loving play

When to push, when to coddle

What you'll notice

As fearless as your child seems on the jungle gym and in spelling bees, he has moments when he appears to wilt. He can be as whiny and needy as when he was 4, constantly demanding your attention or refusing to try. He may also decide that he wants to learn the drums, only to announce that he's quitting because they're "stupid" when you know he's giving up because the lessons are challenging and practising is tedious.

Why it's happening

At this age, your child wants to handle conflicts and problems on his own, but he still depends primarily on adults – especially you – to feel safe. So when things get difficult, he may regress and just want to be your baby again.

Not only is it normal developmentally to take a few steps back, it's common in our fast-paced world. While modern Britain has plenty of advantages – nonstop technology, dozens of TV channels, and lots of after-school activities – these can often make children feel hurried, pressured, and overscheduled. They have so many tempting choices and want to do too many things. The result is that there's often no downtime for them to recharge after their little setbacks, to just laze in their rooms, daydream, or simply work through their frustrations.

How to have fun with it

Start adding some family downtime into every day. Just turn off all the electronics, set a kitchen timer for half an hour, and see what happens. There's no need to do homework, initiate an educational activity or even talk. Make faces or teach him to leg

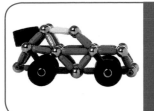

Open-ended projects like magnet building offset scheduled activities.

Did you know?

Trimming your child's calendar now can pay off down the road as he approaches the teen years. According to a recent poll of approximately 900 preteens, 7 out of 10 wished they had more free time (39 per cent were involved in three or more extracurricular activities) and 4 out of 10 said they felt stressed most or all of the time because they had too much to do.

wrestle. Give this half-hour a name – "Do-nothing time" or "Sofa Slouch". When the timer goes off, though, it's back to work, whether that's spelling homework, chores, or piano practice. The break will make you both feel better and closer.

Next, take a hard look at the family calendar: are you expecting your child to do too much? Many experts say children this age should be involved in no more than one activity at a time, yet with so many good programmes available, it's easy to pile karate lessons on top of football. And if there's more than one child in the family, the amount of time kids spend in the car can quickly become excessive. Be brutal, and prune as many activities as you can; ultimately, giving your child more time off will make it easier when you tell him to get down to work.

loving play

Manners matter

What you'll notice

The increased social interactions of Year 3 promise that your child will learn more and more from his pals, and chances are, the behaviour he picks up will not be all good. Children can be very rude to one another, and then come home and try it out on their parents. Eye-rolling, exasperated sighing, simply ignoring you, and clever answers, can become everyday annoyances.

Of course, there's the wonderful flipside – and the opportunity it presents: your 7-year-old is aware when people treat him with rudeness or disrespect, and he doesn't like it one bit. He's also eager to please – a sponge for the compliments guaranteed to come his way when he holds the door for a stranger or thanks the sales assistant at the shop or asks politely to be excused from the table at Granny's house.

Why it's happening

Sociologists can't precisely pinpoint what's behind the surge in bad manners in modern children. Some chalk it up to pop-culture icons that encourage kids to be smart-alecks. Others fault our cultural fascination with self-expression: whether it's on *Pop Idol* or in the playground, blistering rudeness is extolled as a virtue. Most people, though, blame parents. An AP/Ipsos poll found that 93 per cent of Americans think most parents are failing to teach children the most basic manners.

The good news is that this is the Golden Age for the Golden Rule. "How would you feel if someone treated you like that?" penetrates right to the core of a 7-year-old's growing appreciation of fairness. Still smarting from being dissed on the school bus, he can definitely relate to the importance of being polite rather than rude.

How to have fun with it

Few people appreciate kids who are prissy or pretentious. Who cares if your child can't tell the fish fork from the salad fork? But children this age are eager to learn so much more than

Playing it safe

Make sure your child knows when it's okay to be ill-mannered. He should never feel obligated to obey an adult who makes him uncomfortable or frightened.

Writing a note teaches the value of saying "thanks."

"please" and "thank you", especially once they get the basic idea that courtesy is just another way to make other people feel at ease.

Make a game of seeing if your child can guess the reason behind the rule. "Why do we stand to the right on escalators?" (So that people in a hurry can get by without pushing.) "Why do we write a thank-you note when someone invites us over for a nice dinner?" (To let the host know we appreciate how much effort it took.)

Now that your child is probably visiting more friends' homes, talk about observing other families' "house rules", emphasizing the importance of respecting differences. Encourage your child to reciprocate: "I know you like Jimmy's house, because he has a trampoline and two dogs. But it's good manners to invite him here as well."

Children are ready to learn more about mealtime and table manners. Teach him how to set a basic table, with a fork, knife, spoon, plate, napkin, and glass. Play a game of "Dinner with Queen Mean" and eat with exaggerated etiquette, threatening "Off with his head!" when your child puts his elbows on the table.

Make sure your child knows how to shake hands with a grown up, the best way to answer the phone and take a message, and the importance of saying "thanks". These little niceties go a long way toward boosting a child's confidence, especially once they become habitual. Most importantly, practise what you preach. If the man behind you in the queue says something rude about how long your child is taking to order, ask if he'd like to go ahead of you. Taking the high road paves the way for your child's good manners.

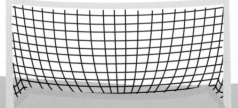

healthy play

Team sports

What you'll notice

Everywhere you look, 7-year-olds are suiting up. Football, baseball, rounders, gymnastics, swimming, and martial arts, there's probably something in your area that will tempt your child, whether it's organized by the school, parent committees, or the local council. At a time when sports and physical education classes in schools are being cut dramatically, the need to get children moving has never been greater.

Why it's happening

This is the perfect time for children, already fired up to socialize in new ways, to join teams. Their physical skills are increasingly sophisticated. For example, her vision has improved enough so that she can really hit a rounders ball. She's able to learn more complex rules, and better equipped emotionally to handle winning and losing.

Children need strenuous activity, say reports by the National Institutes of Health. They're very active, and playing sports allows them to channel their energy. It also satisfies their developmental need to be daring, and while not all like team sports, those who do get plenty of benefits. Obviously, they're more likely to get an adequate amount of exercise than their couch-potato peers, but experts say they gain a sense of confidence in themselves both academically and socially.

How to have fun with it

Shop around for a sport by taking your child to watch kids' games, and see what appeals to her. Talk to her about what she thinks might be fun, what might be scary, and what might be boring. Follow her lead, even if a particular activity might not be your first choice or your

Did you know?

In a number of studies, researchers have found that children with ADHD – even those who have had some bad experiences with sports in the past – can benefit from team involvement, as long as coaches help them catch up on missed skills. Not only does their sports performance improve, so do their peer relationships and happiness levels.

forte. If she seems reluctant, encourage her, and find out which of her friends might be signing up for various programmes; familiar faces can make a new situation less daunting.

If she wants to quit soon after she starts, you can insist she give it another few days. But experts say that while older children do need to understand that joining a team requires a certain commitment, kids this age should be allowed to drop a sport if they don't enjoy it. The reality is that team sports aren't for everyone: some 70 per cent of children will stop playing all organized sports by the time they are 13, according to a Harris Interactive poll. If your child is not a joiner – or particularly interested in sports – help her find less structured fitness activities like walking, running, swimming, biking, dance, or yoga. Above all, observe the team. Make sure every child has a chance to play and that the emphasis is on having a good time.

Sports gear may well supplant toys for an active 7-year-old.

healthy play

Safety first

What you'll notice

With the growing popularity of team sports, and many leagues opening up to younger and younger players, there's also been an increase in sports-related paediatric injuries. The National Institutes of Health says secondary-school-age children involved in organized sports have a one in nine chance of getting injured. Fortunately, most of these injuries are minor – bruises, sprains, strains, and cuts – and do not require medical treatment.

Why it's happening

While more children playing translates into more injuries, there's also been an increase in safety awareness at all levels of kids' athletics. From top sports doctors right down to the average volunteer football coach, adults are keeping a closer eye on

> " My daughter and I do yoga classes together on Saturday mornings and my husband and my son play football. We all get together for brunch afterwards. We all get in our exercise, one-on-one time with the kids, and family time! "
>
> — Betsy, mother of two

how children play. Coaches and physical education teachers routinely incorporate science-based strategies – adequate warming up time, for example, and basic stretching – even at this early age.

Specific risks vary by sport (basketball and gymnastics are among the more injury prone), by size (smaller children shouldn't be matched against much larger children, especially in contact sports like hockey and football), and gender. Researchers at Columbus Children's Hospital recently found that girl football players sustain more injuries than boys, while boys are more likely to have injuries that require hospitalization. Sports doctors have also found girls are between four and eight times more likely to injure their anterior cruciate ligament, or ACL (a knee joint), during team sports.

How to have fun with it

While the idea of an injury can be scary, keep a sense of perspective. For children under 12, sports are very safe, and a fun way for them to get their recommended 60 minutes of daily exercise. The health risks for the many children who don't get enough exercise are considerable. The percentage of children who are overweight has doubled in the past 30 years, and the American Academy of Pediatrics estimates that the typical 7-year-old spends 5½ hours a day watching TV, using computers, and playing video games.

The fitter your child, the healthier he'll be. So make fitness a family affair, by scheduling family walks and bike rides on a regular basis. Even if the coach doesn't seem to encourage it, teach him to warm up before practice and games by jogging in place and doing light stretches. Encourage your child to play more than one sport – maybe football in the autumn, and gymnastics in the winter. That will help him use all muscle groups, and prevent overuse injuries later on.

When shopping for summer programmes, look for camps that include some of the sports he enjoys. Those will help sharpen his skills, prevent injuries, improve his confidence, and expand his circle of friends.

Helmets, kneepads, and the like should be non-negotiable gear for active kids.

healthy play

Beyond the birds and bees

What you'll notice

Watching your child zoom around, it's hard to believe he's thinking much about sex. It's probably been ages since he asked his last vague, "Where do babies come from?" Years ago, experts called this "the latency period", and believed that beginning around age 6, children repressed their interest in sex. Experts now know children have lots of questions about sex, but by the time they turn 6, reports the American Medical Association, they've learned that the issue is private. For instance, they understand that some behaviours aren't socially acceptable, and retreat to the privacy of their bedrooms. Behind closed doors, though, kids this age are still fairly likely to play "Show and Tell" and "Doctor" with one another. They may also express their burgeoning interest in sex by having their dolls act out X-rated scenarios or by making inappropriate "bathroom" jokes.

Why it's happening

Your child's sexual curiosity hasn't gone underground – if anything, he's becoming more sexual, and will continue to do so through adolescence. But he's also picking up on the idea that sex is something that makes adults nervous, so rather than ask the blunt questions so common from younger children, he keeps them to himself, or asks his pals. It's also clear that we live in a world where sexualized images and messages are increasingly ubiquitous. Even if you make a concerted effort to protect your 7-year-old, he may hear sexual terms a lot earlier than you did.

How to have fun with it

Believe it or not, talking about sexuality with your child can actually be fun, once you relax and realize that he just needs to learn the basics with relatively few details. At this age, for example, if you haven't covered where babies come from, try bringing it up again. Experts say your child should have a general idea of how reproduction works, including intercourse, the egg-meets-sperm idea, what a pregnancy is, and how the baby comes out.

Your child is old enough to make the link between healthy food and a healthy body.

Did you know?

Research shows that the average British child can accurately tell you where babies come from by age 9. That's two years earlier than their American counterparts, who know the facts of life by age 11. And 7-year-olds in Sweden know that the stork didn't bring their younger sibling.

Follow his lead, waiting for him to ask additional questions before loading him up with unnecessary (and confusing) tangents.

There are dozens of excellent books about sex aimed at young children which can be very helpful to read together. All of these books emphasize how important it is to avoid cute nicknames for body parts or to combine these pet names with the real names. This is particularly relevant to girls, who, according to research, are far less likely to be taught the anatomical words for their genitals than boys.

A critical goal of any facts-of-life lesson is to communicate to your child a respect for boundaries. Although most children this age are extremely modest, they are also curious. If you discover your child playing "Doctor" with a friend, try not to lose your cool. Later, try to find out how the game got started and whether she was coerced by her friend into playing. Use the

incident as a "teachable moment", to stress that good friends do not pressure one another that way and that "touching games" with an older child or an adult are never, ever okay. Make sure she understands how and when to say no and that she promises to tell you no matter what. One of the best ways to help your child navigate the tricky prepubescent waters is to reinforce her pride in her developing body: talk about how strong and flexible, capable and coordinated she is becoming – positive feelings that will have an indirect but critical impact on her sexuality.

eight- to twelve-year-olds

The Age of Mastery

✳ ✳ ✳

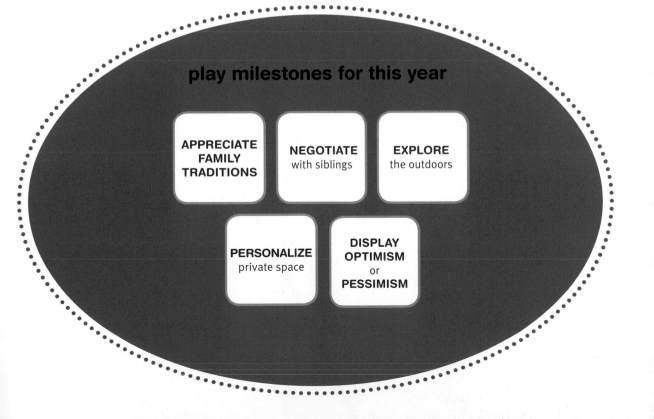

play milestones for this year

APPRECIATE FAMILY TRADITIONS

NEGOTIATE
with siblings

EXPLORE
the outdoors

PERSONALIZE
private space

DISPLAY OPTIMISM
or
PESSIMISM

The Age of Mastery

Some studies have shown that when parents look back, they remember these years with particular warmth. And what's not to love about this parental sweet spot? By age 8, children are able to wash, dress, and feed themselves; most of the time, they even remember to take their vitamins, put their plates in the dishwasher, and their socks in the laundry basket. The higher-conflict teenage years are still out on the horizon and you're guaranteed plenty of loving hugs and enthusiastic conversations.

Meltdowns at this age are for the most part a thing of the past. In their relationships with adults, children are more flexible and accommodating. There are days when they can be downright mellow. As a result, these are years jam-packed with Kodak moments, from spontaneous confidences to memory-making holidays, as your children climb into the car, buckle themselves in, and no longer need countless bathroom breaks.

Family time is vital, and will protect your children for years to come. Researchers have shown that some of the most important factors in raising resilient kids are family celebrations, rituals and routines, and family traditions. And at this age they don't just want to take part in special activities, they want to help plan and create them, knitting your family – including older generations – closer together.

And just as your child's happy enthusiasm can make family life a delight, it's also a joy to watch him take that infectious can-do spirit out into the world. Eight-year-olds are capable of rescuing baby birds, circulating a petition to stop global warming, and surprising you by vacuuming without being asked.

As much as they are growing away from you, they're also growing closer, craving your vote of confidence. Looking for a way to compliment your child? Tell him he's old enough to do the laundry: teach him how to sort clothes, measure detergent, and work the machine. At this age, he doesn't feel burdened; he sincerely wants to help and craves the sense of mastery that a grown-up job provides. In fact, he's so keen on earning your praise that sibling rivalry may flare up. But even these contentious moments will take on a new dimension. Your children still fight, but you will observe them hammering out the ground rules that will govern this important relationship for the rest of their lives.

Negotiation skills and other competencies flourish at school, where children are increasingly encouraged to view their world as a great big science experiment, to ask questions, pose theories, and then figure out the answers. And as they approach double digits, there will be lots of new and tough questions about their changing bodies and dramatic mood swings. Fasten your seatbelt!

learning play

Connecting with nature

What you'll notice

Something's happened to increase your child's level of inquiry. Those sweet, open-ended queries ("Why is the sky blue?" or "Why does water get hard when it's cold?") are replaced by razor-sharp questions: "Which type of clouds make rain?" and "Why does salt water freeze more slowly than fresh?" Schools are harnessing this increase in critical thinking by combining it with hands-on environmental projects, recognizing it as a valuable opportunity to let children know that, as future stewards of the planet, they've got a big job ahead of them. Prepare to be amazed at the level of sophistication and commitment children this age bring to Mother Nature.

Why it's happening

Now that your child is a fluent reader, more seasoned at using her sense of reason, and possesses many analytical abilities (including complex mathematical operations), she's got everything she needs to be a rocket scientist. At school, she's learning to focus on cause and effect; at home, she'll probably think of a few experiments of her own (and create plenty of dirty dishes). That's because she is questioning assumptions. Simply telling her the answer won't be as satisfying as helping her find it herself, and then encouraging her to verify it. Answers like, "Trilobites became extinct before pterodactyls", won't fly, for example. She'll want to know how we know (right down to how carbon dating works on fossils) and why experts think it happened. And the idea that even experts aren't sure (Did asteroids get the dinosaurs? Volcanic activity? Global climate change?) inspires her to ask even more questions.

How to have fun with it

The National Wildlife Foundation recommends that children get a "Green Hour" every day, and that this unstructured time – whether it's spent focusing on an interesting insect, four-leaf clovers, or shells on the beach – is all your budding scientist needs to feel inspired.

Arm your child with a torch and binoculars to explore the outdoors.

Did you know?

Younger children will often say they like all their school subjects and even think they're good at everything, reports a recent study from Humboldt University and the University of Michigan, which tracked 1,000 children from Year 1 to Year 12. But as they get older, they become increasingly special-ized: they not only know which subjects they excel in, but become more likely to say these are also their favourite subjects. Help them identify and pursue their passions – even if they differ from your own.

windowbox gardens and experiment to see whether shade or sunlight produces the tallest tomato plants. Or just before bed-time, wrap up warm and take the whole family outside to see the stars. Some kids are adept at finding constellations and distinct patterns, so if you've got a budding stargazer, telescopes can be great fun, as can joining a local stargazing group.

So send her outdoors. Researchers estimate that children today spend 7½ hours per week more on academics than they did 20 years ago, and 2 hours per week less on sports and outdoor activities. And psychologists have found that more time outdoors makes children happier, healthier, and more alert.

Engage your child's natural curiosity about animals by giving her responsibility for pets and bird feeders, and get her help with planting shrubs and flowers that attract birds and butterflies. Enhance the experience by getting a book that identifies animal species or plant life, and look at things together. Children this age also love to collect and identify shells, so plan a trip to the beach if you can.

Take advantage of the wonderful array of science kits and child-friendly microscopes to look more closely at the treasures she collects on her adventures. If you have a garden, section off a portion that's all hers. Or plant a couple of

learning play

Raising a capable child

2.

1.

What you'll notice

At this age, your child's assessment of his own abilities will vary wildly. One day, he'll assert that he can stay home alone while you go shopping; 15 minutes later, you'll ask him to feed the cat and he'll wail, "I can't make the can opener work. It's too hard."

With some kids, there may be a definite trend: he thinks he can do anything, exhibiting a sense of derring-do that is both admirable and a little scary. (Boys seem more prone to this kind of physical fearlessness, and as a result, National Safe Kids warns that they are three times as likely as girls to injure themselves at school.) Or he may seem easily discouraged, prone to remarks like, "I'm hopeless at sports" or, "None of the kids like me".

Why it's happening

While your child may seesaw between seeing the glass as half full or half empty, most children – like 80 per cent of adults – look on the bright side. You can get a sense of your child's optimism level by the way he explains discouraging events and setbacks in his life.

According to research from the University of Pennsylvania, the hallmarks of pessimism are permanence (he is more likely to say, "My teacher is the meanest ever", rather than, "My teacher is really grumpy today"), pervasiveness ("I'm terrible at maths", rather than, "I am having a hard time with sixes in my times tables"), and personalization, where he places the blame for a problem ("Dad's cross with me because I'm a bad kid", instead of "Dad's ticked off because I forgot to put my bike away").

To a certain degree, how optimistic or pessimistic we are is inherited. But it's also learned. If a mum constantly says, "Oh, I'm so stupid! I always forget to take my keys", chances are her kid will have a more pessimistic outlook – and that's not a good thing.

How to have fun with it

If your child tends toward the pessimistic – or even if he's usually upbeat but having a bad day – experts have found that you can gently help him reframe the way he sees the world. When your child says, "The kids at school never want to play with me", you can reply, "Never? What about yesterday, when you all played together after football practice?" Or when he

Homemade fun

Help children make a sport out of not taking things personally by playing guessing games or making up stories about why a shop assistant or neighbour might have been grumpy: "Maybe her cat has gone missing."

complains, "Kyle didn't invite me to his bowling party – everyone hates me", you can say, "Maybe Kyle couldn't invite you. Remember last year, when you were only able to take eight children roller skating for your birthday?"

More physical games – things like juggling, tae kwon do, or ice-skating – can look nearly impossible at first, but by breaking them down into tiny steps, you can help your child succeed. When you provide ways of making him more optimistic, you promise much more than reduced frustration now; according to research, optimistic people live longer, healthier lives.

The right kinds of games and toys can also help: encourage him to try challenging puzzles or models, which reward his perseverance. And do at least some of it together. A little help from Mum and Dad can go a long way toward helping him feel accomplished.

A puzzle like a Rubik's Cube provides an age-appropriate challenge.

loving play

Sibling rivalry

What you'll notice

Just as your children are more artfully negotiating their social relationships at school, they handle one another at home with more skill. Yes, the inevitable conflicts over who gets to sit where in the car may drive you crazy, but when they come bearing tales of woe ("She's hogging the computer!" or "Mum, he's cheating!"), a disinterested "Hmmm" will probably inspire them to call a truce and figure out a way to keep on playing.

> "We challenge the children to 'parents vs. kids' tournaments – tennis, golf, pool. It's nice to see the little ones working together (even if they make fun of us!) rather than picking on each other."
>
> – Jenny, mother of two

Why it's happening

In the early years, it's easy (well, relatively speaking) for parents to avoid making comparisons between children. But at this stage, when kids are constantly evaluating how they measure up at school and on the athletic field, they manufacture their own rankings at a mind-boggling rate – and someone always winds up on the bottom. These comparisons become particularly fierce at home, where the fact that one sibling is better at schoolwork, has more friends, or excels at ballet can exacerbate the rivalry. And because children this age value social relationships more and more, they may show off to their friends by dissing their siblings: "That's my stupid sister – pay no attention to her." Of course, should one of the friends choose to pick on Baby Sis, the first person to jump to her defence will probably be her older brother or sister.

How to have fun with it

One way to get kids to cooperate more (and squabble less) is to give them more autonomy, challenging them to solve problems on their own. Feign deafness whenever possible. Researchers have found that kids who are allowed to work the kinks out of their sibling relationships learn skills that prove critical in later adult connections.

As well as consciously avoiding the referee role, you can foster a sense of teamwork by asking your children to do the weekend chores together instead of delegating. Or ask them to come up with a week's worth of dinner menus or a list of five possible holiday destinations.

Channel your children's competitive spirit into family fun. Split up into teams for games that all ages enjoy – not just board games and card games, but also parlour games like Charades and Botticelli.

While you may have to step in from time to time when putdowns get out of hand, you can also use their "Game on!" attitude to get more cooperation: "The politest person this week gets a visit to the ice cream shop", for example, rewards family harmony, instead of inspiring more cut-throat competition.

Games that both siblings can play, like a bat and ball, are good for combating sibling rivalry.

loving play

Privacy, please

What you'll notice

One day, you'll walk upstairs while your normally uninhibited daughter is changing, and she'll slam the door, with a prudish, "Do you mind?" You'll ask how school is, only to hear a monosyllabic "Fine", and you might even get a preview of the classic preteen freeze-out – a "Keep out" sign on her door. Phone conversations with her pals will take place out of earshot of Mum or Dad and her "stuff" will be sacrosanct – especially when one of her siblings asks to borrow something.

Why it's happening

From the first time she crawled away from you, your child has been exploring ways to separate. And, yes, it can be sad, even hurtful, when your 10-year-old shrugs off your arm or retreats to her room the minute she gets home. Although that shut-out feeling can lead many parents to pry and be overly invasive, keep in mind that all children this age need emotional and mental space as much as they do physical privacy.

The good news is that 8-, 9-, even 10-year-olds still feel very close to their parents, and while they may push you away, they don't want you to go very far. Laying down clear, consistent rules and boundaries about everything from computers to TV to homework to family time will make your child feel protected, safe, and valued – even if she protests that you're the strictest parent on the planet.

How to have fun with it

Let your child know that you respect her growing need for privacy – and look for new ways to support it. Encourage her to write in a diary or to keep a journal. Physically, she may

> ### Homemade fun
>
> What better way to keep a secret than invisible ink? Show your child how to write on plain paper using lemon juice and a cotton swab. After it dries, illuminate it with a lightbulb, iron, or heating pad.

want to carve out her own space: a fort or treehouse in the backgarden can be a great family project. Or let her personalize her room to make it feel more like a retreat. But do not put a TV or computer in her room. Studies have shown that children who do have televisions in their bedrooms run the risk of becoming seriously overweight. They also tend to get less sleep per week, which can compromise their health. Limit TV, computer, or video game time to two hours maximum per day.

As far as her emotional privacy is concerned, switch strategies. Try to schedule some alone time together. Maybe it's a Sunday shopping trip or the Friday night pizza run. Sure, your child may clam up, but when she wants or needs to talk, she'll know you're there.

Boys, in particular, are likely to open up during play, so make time for a kickabout or play a board game together. Fortunately, most children this age are in constant need of chauffeurs and find the protective dark of the car conducive to sharing personal information. Simple chores – folding the laundry together, for example – provide the same kinds of opportunities.

A journal is a perfect vehicle for a preteen to record her private thoughts and feelings.

healthy play

Body image

What you'll notice

As early as 8, but certainly by 11, your child will show signs of puberty. While some children are totally oblivious to these changes, others become painfully self-conscious. Some hide behind baggy clothes and even refuse to go to the beach or pool. In fact, one study found that 80 per cent of girls, in Years 3 to 6, have had bad feelings about their bodies. Others seem to turn into overnight teenagers, obsessed not just with their own clothes and looks, but also with fashions in books, dolls, computers, TV, and films.

> "One night my daughter stumbled onto a few pictures of me taken during my incredibly awkward adolescence. I could see that she was highly amused – as well as comforted by the fact that I had survived.
>
> – Patty, mother of one

Why it's happening

Some of these transitions are inevitable, but many of the changes are brought on by a culture that places far more value on the way a girl looks than on her inner beauty. In fact, experts fear this sexualization – urging girls to think that being "hot" is the only thing that matters – is reaching epidemic proportions. The American Psychological Association recently assigned a task force on the subject, and experts have linked the way young girls identify with excessively sexy singers, TV and movie characters, and fashions with depression, low self-esteem, and with eating disorders in children as young as 8. What's more, researchers have found that, especially for girls, these body-image problems are, to a degree, contagious: the more her friends focus on achieving the perfect body, the more she will too.

How to have fun with it

The more children move their bodies, the more they like them. So while it's important to encourage them to sign up for sports and activities, it's also fun to build in family time that is active and unstructured. Family walks before dinner, weekend outings to the beach, and impromptu dance-a-thons all help.

Provide healthy-body realities to counter the emaciated fantasies she sees in the media. Teach children about eating well, which can protect against obesity as well as eating disorders. Include them in food shopping and cooking, which teaches about nutrition, and also make sure they're getting at least ten hours of shut-eye every night.

Most importantly, celebrate her unique talents – whether it's skateboarding or making jewellery. If she seems to be struggling with her self-image, pair her up with younger children who will probably hang on her every word and make her more aware of the many gifts she has to share.

Encourage your child to explore a hobby like jewellery making in order to feel good about herself.

Index

Acknowledgments

The author wishes to thank Sarah Mahoney, Michele Bender, and Laura Lacy for their assistance with research and writing. And a special thanks to Charles Koppelman, who was the inspiration for this book. Downtown Bookworks would like send special thanks to Patty Brown, Sarah Parvis, and Number 17. Thanks to the following children who modelled for this book:

Lucy Abrams
Marta Abrams
Nyrah André
Jonathan Bender
Sofia Bhatti
Ruby Bromberg
Esther Bullock
Simon Bullock
Jonas Cruz
Tiana Davis
Jackson Deysine
Lucas Deysine
Avery Dollard
Imogen Gifford
Maizy Glassman
Jasper Ming Gruswitz
Elijah Haylett
Emmanuel Haylett
Hannah Kaplan
Kal Katz
Morris Katz
Nathanael Katz
Joaquin Kull
Téa Kuzbari
Sophia Lam
Adam Lane
Justin Lee
Kaya Leitner
Sophia Leitner

Maya Lubetsky
Jahmal Marajah
Simon Marshall
Miles Matthews
Ashira Mawji
Daelum Mawji
Romeo Michelson
Madison Mobray
Claire Niumata
Mia Platoni
Hailey Ramondo
Nicholas Ramondo
Alexander Reddish
Lucas Romero
Sierra Romero
Nessa Schmitt
Kyle Song
Bella Steinberg
Josiah Stevens
Tsion Stevens
Roberto Cesar Vidal
Ava Villalba
Maia Villalba
Paris White
Jalen Wright
Quentin Wright
Thomas Yi